Dear Breast Cancer,

Thank you for the lemons, I'm making lemonade.

Lolita Jackson

ISBN-13: 9798857352472
ISBN 10: 1477123456

Cover design by: Dominic Harris
Library of Congress Control Number: 2018675309
Printed in the United States of America

Table Of Contents

Lolita Jackson is a Breast Cancer Badass. We went through Breast Cancer Badass %*#! together.
Lolita Jackson made me a Breast Cancer Badass, taking lemons and making lemonade.
Stephen Jackson

"Lolita, my daughter, attend to my words; incline your ear

unto my sayings. Let them not depart from your eyes;

keep them in the midst of your heart, Lolita. For they are

life unto those who find them and health to all their flesh.

Lolita, wisdom is the principal thing; therefore, get wisdom;

and with all your getting, get understanding. Exalt wisdom,

Lolita, and she shall promote you and your health as she

brings you honor when you embrace her. Do not forsake

her, Lolita, and wisdom will preserve you, love you, and

keep you. Lolita, now is the time to take fast hold of

instruction and don't let it go; keep her, for wisdom is

your life. Ponder the path of your feet, Lolita, and let all of

your ways be established. Lolita, it's time that you hear

my instruction as your Father and attend to know

understand, for now, I am giving you good doctrine.

Lolita, please do not forsake my law; let your heart retain my

words, keep my commandments, and live. Lolita, now is

the time; you must get wisdom, get understanding: do not forget it

nor decline from the words of my mouth. Lolita, my

beloved daughter, keep your heart with all diligence; for out

of your heart are the issues of life. You are just, and

your path is as a shining light that shines more and more

unto the perfect day."

"Proverbs 4:20-23"

I AM THAT	I AM THAT	I AM THAT	I AM THAT
Lion	*Healed*	*Courage*	*Almighty*
I AM	I AM	I AM	I AM

I AM THAT	I AM THAT	I AM THAT	I AM THAT
Savage	*Omniscience*	*Confidence*	*Warrior*
I AM	I AM	I AM	I AM

I AM THAT	I AM THAT	I AM THAT	I AM THAT
Power	*Bold*	*Beast*	*Life*
I AM	I AM	I AM	I AM

I AM THAT	I AM THAT	I AM THAT	I AM
Jaguar	*Awesome*	*One*	*Discipline*
I AM	I AM	I AM	THAT I AM

I AM THAT	I AM THAT	I AM THAT	*Strength* AND *Fearless*
Eagle	*Alive*	*Fierce*	I AM
I AM	I AM	I AM	

I AM THAT	I AM	I AM THAT	I AM THAT
Fight	*Truth*	*Lionhearted*	"*Bad Ass*"
I AM	THAT I AM	I AM	I AM

6

Testimonies

Reflections on a Journey

Watching a loved one grapple with a grave diagnosis is a profound and heart-wrenching experience, especially when that individual is one's own mother. As her daughter, witnessing her confront breast cancer was a poignant reminder of the unpredictability of life. The malady did not arise from any action, word, or choice of hers. Yet, it relentlessly challenged her womanhood and spirit.

On three distinct occasions, I watched as she faced the disheartening news of the cancer's recurrence. Each time, the weight of the words seemed insurmountable: an initial diagnosis, a return on the other side, and a later spread to her lymph nodes. Many would have been crushed by the magnitude of such repeated setbacks. Yet, my mother stood undeterred. Her journey wasn't merely one of survival; it was a testament to unparalleled determination, resilience, and indomitable faith. Through it all, she exhibited an elegance, grace, and gratitude that was nothing short of awe-inspiring.

My mother transformed an ordeal laden with bitterness into a narrative of hope, faith and joy, making the best out of an extremely challenging situation. To say she is a warrior is an understatement. She's a beacon of light, vulnerabilities and strength. I am filled with boundless pride and honor to be her daughter.

With deepest admiration,
Mary Paschal, Daughter

Mom,

In life, some words bear a weight so profound that they alter the very fabric of one's existence. One such word for me is CANCER. Its mere mention remained distant, until the day its shadow darkened our doorstep. I recall the quiet dread in my parents' eyes, the hushed tones, as they gently unveiled to me that my mother, my rock, was diagnosed with breast cancer.

Each day, I bore witness to a battle of spirit and of hope against despair. As her son, seeing her weakened was daunting, yet her unyielding tenacity showcased the essence of her faith and beliefs. Thrice she faced the specter of this disease, and thrice she emerged triumphant. Amidst these tumultuous times, she inspired me to honor my commitments, to persist through my educational journey, sports while trying to maintain a childhood with some sort of normality trying to mirror her unyielding tenacity.

To label her merely as a survivor feels inadequate. She's a beacon of enduring strength, a testament to the indefatigable human spirit. To the disease that dared challenge her: know that you contended with an indomitable force, and she bested you, time and again. In the face of adversity, my mother personified the very essence of fortitude.

Breast Cancer, you attempted to shake the foundation of our family, but you were met with a resolute warrior. And you were defeated.

With unwavering pride and respect,

Sir Stephen Jackson, Son

Fierce Tenacity, Grit & Grace

Witnessing my sister's confrontation with cancer brought forth a myriad of emotions. From the moment she received her diagnosis, my instinct was to dive deep, to research, to explore every avenue of treatment and care — only to find that she had preemptively taken those steps herself. That's just who she is, my big sister, always one step ahead, always grabbing life by the horns, never allowing challenges to steer her off course.

Throughout her journey, I've watched her embrace surgery after surgery with unmatched valor, turning every setback into an opportunity. True to her spirit, she transformed the bitterness of her experience into a source of inspiration, both literally and metaphorically.

While undergoing chemotherapy and its subsequent recovery phases, she founded a lemonade stand, infusing humor and diligence into her ordeal. And as if her courage wasn't radiant enough, she brought her signature style to every hospital stay, adorning her space with her vibrant energy. She firmly believes that when you look good and smell good, you feel good — and she embodied this mantra every step of the way.

From doctor's appointments to early morning surgeries, she always presented herself with meticulous care, ensuring even her sparse hair moments were nothing short of fabulous.

If I were to encapsulate her essence during these trying times, the word would undoubtedly be 'FIERCE'. Her fierce determination, fierce style, and fierce spirit shone through. Yet, her strength never overshadowed her vulnerable frailties as a woman stricken with an awful diagnosis while faced with unimaginable decisions and choices to make. She allowed her fears and apprehensions to surface, but they never dominated. Instead, her immense fortitude and can-do attitude took precedence, inspiring all of us around her. To my sister, whose tenacity astounds me every day, I am endlessly proud and grateful for your love, life and laughter!

With all my love,
Kimberly Swopes-Washington, Sister

Dear Breast Cancer,
thank you for the
lemons,
I'm making lemonade

INTRODUCTION

My name is Lolita Jackson. I am a three-time Breast Cancer Overcoming Badass! It's been a long and difficult process to complete book one of a three-book trilogy where I will share my different experiences on this long and winding road to recovery and restoration. In this book, I do my best to capture the initial raw, gut-wrenching feelings of hearing that I had breast cancer for the first time.

It's August , 2023. It has taken me 15 years and 11 months to publish this book. It's not easy; there are some things that I share that are so personal that I feel raw, naked, and exposed before the world. And I'm not just talking about my body, even though that's part of it. I am talking about my feelings, my emotions, the vulnerability in sharing, and yes, caring. Caring enough that I don't want one more person in this world to experience breast cancer or any other cancer and feel like they're alone and hopeless. My hope and desire, as I bare my soul, is that whether it is breast cancer or cancer in general, you know that you're strong, you can do this, and you've got this. I want you to know that if Lolita Jackson can get through cancer three times, you too can make it. I want to say: don't give up on yourself! I am writing this to say: FIGHT! And when you put your boxing gloves down at the end of the day, LAUGH, SMILE, WRITE, SCRIPT, and most of all, LOVE YOURSELVES.

I know it's tough. I also know that this is probably one of the toughest things that you'll have to deal with if you're the one who has the diagnosis or the one that's supporting a loved one with the diagnosis. Together, we will make it; together, you can make it. I Love You, your friend and Cancer Champ Companion, Lolita Jackson.

Without further ado, it is with great pleasure and humility that I offer you this book as a

testament to courage, strength, and resilience in the face of a disease that affects millions of

women and families around the world. The disease of breast cancer and its diagnosis can be devastating. The journey of treatment and recovery is filled with challenges, both physical and emotional.

But in the face of all these difficulties, I found the strength and courage to rise above the storm with eagle wings and emerge stronger on the other side.

My book is a collection of my stories and insights as a woman who has been through the fire of breast cancer myself. I write this book as a tribute to all women and families of women who have faced the disease of Breast Cancer and come out on the other side with newfound strength, hope, and determination. This book is for you. It is a powerful reminder that no matter how difficult life may become, this too shall pass; there is always hope for a brighter tomorrow. I invite you to dive into the pages of this inspiring book and discover the stories of courage and resilience that lies within.

Sincerely,
Lolita Jackson

INTRODUCTION ADJACENT

(I know I made this up, smile)

I can't proceed with the publishing and release of this book without addressing something crucial. What I'm about to say encompasses everything—yes, everything—related to your diagnosis, treatment, recovery, and survival.

Here it is... I'm about to preach...

I don't care what anyone—did you hear me say anyone? I mean anyone—says to you regarding your diagnosis. The only thing that matters is what you say to yourself; that's all that matters, period

(I know it's not grammatically correct, trust me, but when you're going through this fight, being grammatically correct is the last thing on your mind, so it doesn't matter what anyone thinks.)

Now, let me explain why I needed an 'introduction adjacent' for this book. When you go through something as traumatic as cancer, you'll receive advice and comments from all directions and from everyone.

Most people have the best of intentions, but sometimes you may feel compelled to take all the advice and comments to heart. Don't! Instead, take in the useful information and discard the rest.

17

Your healing begins the moment you affirm who and what you are to yourself. It's here that I started scripting intensely. Write down what you want and create the reality you desire.

When you're alone and looking in the mirror, the only person standing there is you. It's behind closed doors where you must say "I AM," followed by your desired outcome. Your mirror is your vision board. Regardless of what you see in the mirror at the time, speak to yourself as if you have already achieved your desired outcome. Declare it through tears, loneliness, and even through the hardships. This is where, even if you feel weak, you say "I AM STRONG!" Every word you utter is your power in action. This is where you find stillness, acknowledge your strength, and express

gratitude. Your prayers are answered through your belief in the outcome.

PART TWO: FORGET PART TWO IF YOU DON'T BELIEVE PART ONE...

You must believe in your "I AM" script as if you were writing a script for a movie, knowing the outcome. If you envision yourself healed, then declare "I AM HEALED!" every day in every way.

Now, embody that belief and write it out.

What does that look like? (BEAUTIFUL)

What does that sound like? (ALL THINGS POSITIVE, BIRDS CHIRPING—OPEN YOUR EARS AND YOU'LL HEAR THEM)

I am healed; I am the resurrection and the life.

What does that feel like? (LOVE, ABUNDANCE, PEACE, TRANQUILITY, WATER) Feel it.

Where are you? If you imagine yourself by the water, then place yourself there in your

imagination, where your power resides. Delve deep beyond your veil. There, you will find your happy place, your sacred space. It is there; it is here. Your beauty for ashes, your rose of Sharon, your Lily of the valley. You're the only one who has paid the price and knows the cost of the anointing oil in your alabaster box.

I LOVE YOU,

Lolita

P.S.
I have included some blank scrolls for you to script your very own I AM Affirmations…

19

Surprise

Surprise

Surprise

Another name for God is surprise.

~Brother David Steindl – Rast

1.UNEXPECTED

As I lay on the examination table in the doctor's office, you would have never believed that this was my first time meeting my doctor by the way we were laughing with one another, talking like old friends reacquainted as if we had known each other all our lives. It was a routine gynecological exam, nothing out of the ordinary. The doctor asked me the standard questions that a patient would expect on a first-time visit. I was at the gynecologist's office for a well-woman care visit. The exam was going quite well, and I was thinking I would be there for a maximum of 15 minutes. The doctor let the exam table recline backwards and proceeded with her examination, probing and asking the pertinent questions that a doctor would ask. I answered, telling her that I was feeling great, with no problems, but then I thought about it and said, "Well, I have been having chest pains."

The doctor was at the lower part of my body doing what a doctor does at the lower part of a woman's body at the gynecologist's office. She looked up at me and asked, "How often do you feel the pain?" Not thinking anything of it, I said, "All of the time." I told the doctor that the pain was constant and that it never went away. I told her that it was on the left side of my chest and that there were times when the pain was so severe that I would go to the emergency room. I also told her that the pain wasn't caused by exertion. I told her that there would be times when I would be sitting watching television, reading a book, or be awakened out of my sleep because of the pain. She wanted me to describe the pain. I told her that it was a constant burning sensation, that it would throb, and at times it would feel like a stabbing or like acupuncture needles were being pushed into my chest. I told the doctor that I had been to the hospital so many times due to this pain in my chest that I felt like the hospital was tired of seeing me. I told the doctor that I was admitted to the hospital a couple of months earlier and that they did an angiogram and put a stent in my arteries to see if I was having heart problems, but all of my tests came back normal. I told the doctor that I had had too many EKGs to count because every time I had gone in and told them my chest was hurting, they had to check my heart to no avail. I then said to the doctor, "But that's another problem for another day; my chest pains have nothing to do with a gynecological appointment."

The doctor never said another word. She methodically worked her way to the upper part of my body and told me to raise my arms above my head and point to where the pain was coming from in my chest. I pointed

to the area on the left side of my chest where my left breast was. I then

told her that it seemed to be radiating. As I was talking, she gave me the

breast exam that women receive when they go to the gynecologist's office

for their annual well-woman care appointment. I didn't think anything of

it until the countenance on her face changed.

It was at that moment that her smile went away, her eyes

seemed to sink to the back of her eye sockets. I saw it, that look with

my own two eyes – it was a look of fear, dreadful and frightening.

Immediately, nothing was funny anymore. She gave me one of those

forced, half-smiles that she thought was a full smile, but it wasn't. At

that moment, my life changed, little did I know how much my life

would change and why it would change. Suddenly, the atmosphere in

the room changed. I swear, I felt a cold shiver go through my body.

Why did the room get so cold? Why was I freezing? Why was

everything so dark and eerie? I didn't know.

As the doctor continued examining my breast, she now had this

intense, concerned, "Oh my goodness, you poor thing" demeanor

about her. I started asking questions to fill the room with words to

break the deafening silence that gave me the chills.

"What's wrong?" I asked. I wanted her to talk to me. I was thinking, why is she touching me so much and so deeply? In my mind, I said to her, "Hello, Doctor, are you there? Say something, please, I can't take it anymore." I didn't say anything aloud, though; I read the room and felt the energy that spoke to me, telling me to be quiet and let the doctor examine me. Then the silence broke, and the doctor said, "Lolita, give me your hand. I want you to feel this area of your breast with the tips of your fingers. Do you feel that?"

I gave her my fingers, and with her hand over mine, she guided my fingers over my left breast. I felt something in my breast; it was firm and felt like a knot. It reminded me of when I was a little girl when my breast started to grow. The first feeling was this firm knot, a ball-like sensation inside my chest, my breast. I could feel the knot, the ball-like substance, but at this point in the exam, it wasn't registering to me that it could mean anything other than something being there and me touching where I felt pain. Of course, my touch wasn't a soft, tender one. Oh no, it was deep – her hand was pressing my hand and fingers into my skin and around this knot in my breast. She wanted me to really feel what she had felt; she wanted me to know that something was going on, and her face showed her concern. I told her, "Yes, I do feel it." I then said, "It's hard, it's big, wow, what is it?" The doctor replied, "Well, we need to take a look at it. I want you to go down the hall to the mammography clinic, and I will call and let the receptionist at the clinic know that I'm sending you to have a mammogram and an ultrasound. I want to see you immediately afterward with the results."

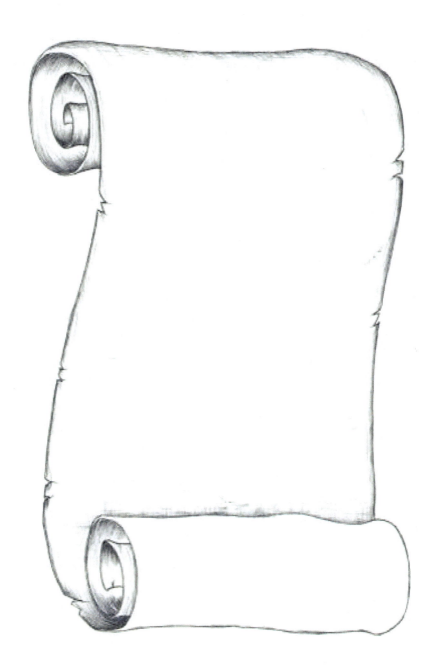

2. UNSETTLED

That was a long walk; it seemed like it took hours and miles to walk down and across the hall to the mammography clinic. The receptionist was expecting me and knew my name. They got me right in, which I found nice since it hardly ever happens that quickly. I removed my upper garments, again, and proceeded to have a mammogram. The mammogram machine is big and scary-looking. The room was cold, lights were dim, a bit ominous, I must say. They were specific about what they wanted to see. The nurse took my breast into her hands and placed it flat on a tray that looked almost like a specimen tray, just a little larger. She told me to lift my arm up as she pressed down on top of my breast with the machine that reminded me of a hydraulic machine. It was excruciating, so I called for God in my mind. It truly was very painful. My face showed a grimace, but she wasn't finished because she needed to show images from several angles. This time, they smashed my breast and chest flat against the cold plate on that big machine and pressed some more. "Wow," I thought, "you've got to be kidding me." Next, I needed to have the ultrasound.

The ultrasound tech was quiet, and the room was dark. She put gel on the tip of the wand in her hand and pressed it into my breast while moving it back and forth, taking pictures. She moved the little round ball on the machine, clicking away and pressing into my breast deeper and deeper. I was still in a lot of pain; however, I was calm, cool, and nonchalant about what was going on, thinking it was just a procedure, right? I returned to the doctor's office and they led me back to the same room I was in prior.

The doctor came in and asked, "What did they say, Lolita? How did it go?"

"Doc, I'm fine, it's just fatty tissue. My breasts are dense; even the specialist, the radiologist herself, said the same thing that the technician said. Have no fear, doctor; it's okay. I'll see you a year from now."

"Ugh, oh." There she goes again with that look. I thought to myself, why is she looking through me? Her eyes and energy couldn't hide the eeriness I was feeling. "Stop that, you're making me nervous; besides, don't worry, you should be happy. You have the report in your hands. These people are professionals; they know what they're talking about, right?" As I continued to have this internal dialogue with myself. Keep in mind, this was one of the nicest doctors I have had the pleasure of meeting; however, I was picking up on something I didn't want any part of... This new doctor lady was never going to see me again; I couldn't wait to get out of her office.

As the doctor was talking, I realized I couldn't figure out what she was saying. I don't know when it happened, but I zoned out for a few seconds; my spirit was off, our connection had been violated, and I continued to feel that energy of what I'll call "deep concern." I looked up into her eyes and heard her say, "Lolita, I know what the report says, but I don't believe it."

I was sitting there, motionless and perplexed, wondering what this doctor was saying to me. You see, I believe in speaking things into existence and calling those things that are not as if they were, and if I do say something that is wrong or negative, I believe in taking it out of the atmosphere, so it doesn't manifest. So for the doctor to be telling me she doesn't believe the report, then obviously So she's believing the opposite, and right now at this very moment, I'm not trying to believe you, Miss Doctor Lady, and I sure as hell am not trying to hear anything you're talking about right now. "Damn it!" I thought to myself.

I said, "Excuse me, you don't believe it? Why not?" I just looked at her.

Then I heard her say, "Lolita, I want to do a biopsy on the lump."

Now the fatty tissue is a lump? This lady is crazy, and I am getting out of here on the next thing smokin!

So I said to the doctor, "You mean the fatty tissue, right?"

She was confusing me; it sounded like she was talking in another language. I don't hear or use words like lumps, mammograms, and biopsies.

"Yes, the fatty tissue," she said, trying to smile.

She explained what a biopsy procedure consisted of. She went on to tell me that she wanted to do it right there in the room that day. She explained that she was going to take a long needle, put it in the lump, extract some of the tissue from the middle of it, and send it to the lab to see if it is benign or not. "Benign?" There she goes again, speaking in that language, talking that funny stuff.

"Benign, okay, Doc, what's going on here?" I was thinking this in my mind. "Lolita, I'm concerned about the lump, and I want to rule out any possibility of it being cancerous!"

"Say what?" I was stunned; there's no way! Now, I'm really out of here. "What about it just being fatty tissue?" I asked. Before I could exhale as I took a breath to inhale, I was taking off my clothes from the waist up, again, and the doctor was laying all these medical supplies out on the counter that looked like surgical supplies, as if she was about to do surgery. I remember the gloves as she snapped them on her hand. The noise seemed to be especially loud. I was looking at her from behind, thinking, "Please don't turn around with a monster face." She put on a yellow lab coat, took out the tools, placed them on a silver tray. I saw a long needle with a large round circle at the end of it. She turned around with a mask, her gloves, and that lab coat, with her tray placed on a table next to us, and proceeded closer to me in her chair. I was now face to face with her and this long needle in her gloved hand pointed at me.

The only thing I could think of at that moment was, "Oh, shit!" The doctor put some iodine on my breast to clean the area of penetration, then rubbed alcohol, and stuck the needle in my breast. I didn't hear her say, "Brace yourself, this may hurt a little, take a deep breath," or anything.

I felt this pain from hell and could hear a loud clicking noise. Tears started to roll down my face. I began to cry, I couldn't hold back the tears, even though I tried, I really, really did try. I wasn't going to let her or another doctor see me cry. I was hurting inside, I was still hurting from the previous doctor's disbelief in the source of my pain, I was hurting inside and it all came out at that very moment. Everything was happening so fast. I was thinking, "How did I get here, and who is this woman?"

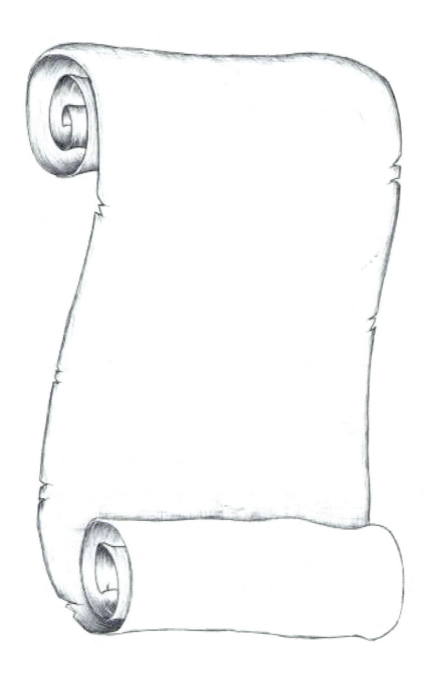

3. WAIT

I got dressed, and the next two days were the longest days of my life. My appointment was early in the morning. I wanted to go first thing because I wouldn't be able to sit around all day waiting.

"Mrs. Jackson, the doctor will see you now."

I smiled at the receptionist, trying to read her. I wanted to know if she knew something about me that I didn't know. Would she smile back with a smile as bright as the sun, or would she give me the fake, forced "OMG, you poor thing" smile? Because I can read people, you know? (Smile) "Okay, Doc, what are the results of the biopsy?"

"Lolita, your biopsy results show that you have tested positive for ductal in situ carcinoma."

I looked at her, and her lips were moving, but I didn't HEAR anything else she was saying. I promise I heard nothing. Before that moment, I'm not sure that I knew what the word carcinoma meant, but for some reason, instantly I knew that carcinoma meant cancer. I just knew it. However, if for some reason I was wrong, after the doctor's lips stopped moving, I asked her - I mean, I reaffirmed the meaning of the word carcinoma.

I said, "So, I have cancer? You mean I have breast cancer?"

She said, "Yes."

Then she leaned over the table toward me to show me what was on the paper. I stopped her and went out to the lobby to call for my husband to come into the room.

I said, "Will you please explain to my husband everything you just said to me? I need to call my sister and my daughter so they can be on the phone to hear what you're about to say." As I sat there, tears that started out as little trickles down my cheeks turned into a spring of showers. I became numb and despondent. All I had the strength to do was cry. I could hear the shock and awe in my sister and daughter's voices. I let them ask all the questions, I had no words, absolutely zero. The doctor told me that she wanted me to go downstairs in order to have an MRI.

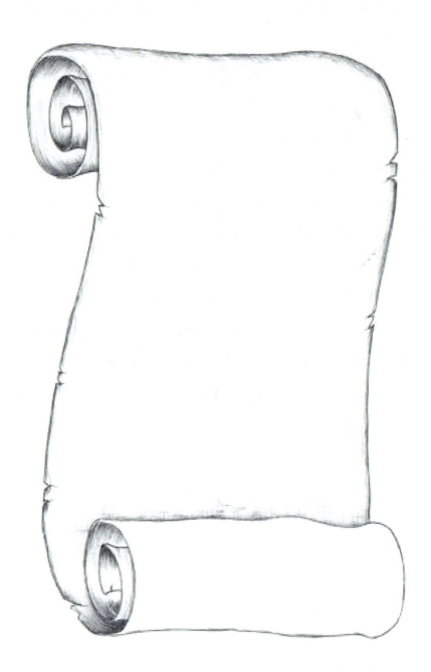

4. STEADFAST

The MRI will show us more images so we can gauge the length, width, and depth of the tumor."

I walked into the room where I was going to have my MRI. The lady who was to take my images was friendly; I felt safe, and she played music. I had taken a valium before the procedure, so I was as relaxed as I could be.

"Mrs. Jackson, wake up, we're done, your procedure is over."

It wasn't that warm, fuzzy lady; it was someone else who was cold and bitter. "Let's get this IV out of your arm and get you out of here."

As I was leaving, I saw the warm, fuzzy lady. My spirits lifted, hoping to make eye contact with her lively, cozy, delicious aura of juicy kindness and perfect joy, only to have her deliberately turn away as if I was the ebola lady, quickly turn your head away from her, lady, the don't look up at her, lady, because I just saw her MRI, and I see she's not whole, or worse, the tumor is enormous at 9 1/2 centimeters lady, the there's no way she will survive from what I'm seeing on these images lady. The lady is looking at my inevitable fate of doom, lady. I felt the cool breeze of her cold dismissal while getting a glance of the picture image on the monitor. The desk she was sitting at had a picture of my breast, all perfect and beautiful, with this grayish, whitish, long thing in the middle. I started thinking to myself, "OMG, is that it? Is that the tumor? Is that what the cancer in me looks like? Whoa! It's huge, it's long and fatty, it's not some dense fat. It's real, and I see it's there. There it is, cancer."

The "C" word. The reason my life has been turned upside down for the last couple of days. I started to think to myself again. "Should I say something to the fuzzy lady?" "Should I just stick my head in the door and ask if I could take a closer look at the image?" "Should I say, OMG, hey fuzzy lady, is that image real?" What should I do if she won't even look up at me? I have the plague now, or, what is it, lady? Please, this is hard enough as it is; please don't dismiss me, not now. The fuzzy lady was like me when I first heard the word carcinoma referring to me, Lolita Jackson.

She was numb and speechless, sitting there thinking, "How do I look into this lady's face with a straight face knowing that the image I see is massive?" No one can survive a tumor 9 1/2 centimeters in length and 3' in depth. So, she never looked up, and I never said a word. I went to my car with that image embedded in my mind to this day.

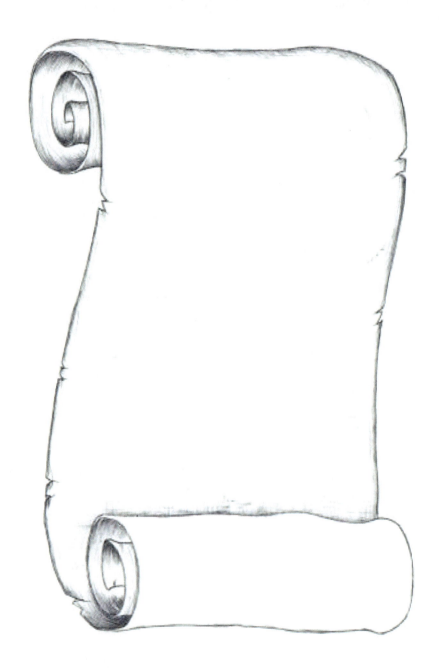

5. GRACE

I got home after the MRI and went to the mailbox, three days after I was diagnosed with ductal in situ carcinoma and after having a mammogram on the same day. I opened a letter from the breast clinic that said, "Dear Mrs. Jackson, thank you for coming into the breast clinic and having your annual mammogram. Your test is normal, and we look forward to seeing you next year at the hospital." It was at that minute that I knew how thankful I am! If I hadn't trusted my doctor and if my doctor would've believed the report. I'm glad she followed through with her gut feelings to challenge the fatty tissue, dense breast diagnosis and do a biopsy that rendered a confirmation of ductal in situ carcinoma.

And because of that, the cancer was found early enough to be treated, thus the title:

"Dear Breast Cancer, Thank You for the lemons, I'm making lemonade!"

As I held the letter in my hands, I couldn't help but feel an overwhelming wave of gratitude. It was a strange sensation, thanking something as devastating as breast cancer. But in that moment, I realized how fortunate I was to have a doctor who trusted her instincts and pushed for further examination. I started thinking about the ride home, it was a contemplative one. I thought about the rollercoaster of emotions I had experienced in such a short time - the fear, the uncertainty, the relief.

All of it led me to this moment, where I could genuinely say, "Thank you, breast cancer." It was a reminder to trust my instincts and the professionals who were there to help me. Because of their diligence and expertise, my cancer was caught early, and I had the chance to fight back. I knew that from this day forward, I would never take my health for granted. This experience has taught me the importance of regular check-ups and listening to my body. As I stepped through the front door of my home, I felt a renewed sense of purpose and determination. I was facing the unknown, and I was ready for whatever challenges life had in store for me.

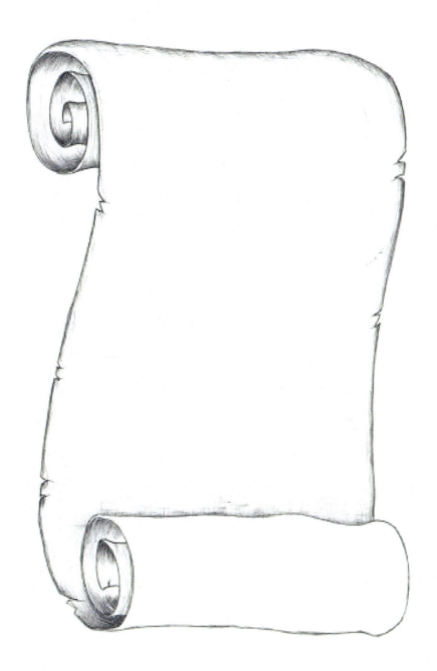

6. GRATITUDE

The first step in maintaining a positive outlook after a breast cancer diagnosis is to understand what it means. Educate yourself about the type of breast cancer you have, the stage of your cancer, and the treatment options available to you. Knowledge is power, and the more you know about your diagnosis, the more in control you will feel.

One of the most important things you can do after a breast cancer diagnosis is to connect with others who have gone through the same thing.

Joining a support group or connecting with other survivors can provide you with the emotional support you need. Setting goals can help you stay focused and motivated during your breast cancer journey. However, it's important to set realistic goals that take into account your physical and emotional limitations. Setting small, achievable goals can help you feel a sense of accomplishment and boost your mood. Finally, celebrating milestones can help you maintain a positive outlook throughout your breast cancer journey.

This might involve celebrating the end of treatment, reaching a new goal, or simply taking time to acknowledge how far you've come.

Celebrating milestones can help you stay motivated and hopeful for the future.As for me, I knew instantly that I would start keeping a daily account of everything I was thankful for. In the midst of my tears and fears, I was determined to be grateful and mindful of everything. That was the only way I was going to make it through this diagnosis. But now, how do I find joy amidst the pain? How do I deal with my tears and fears? How do I process all of this stuff that was happening to me? The answers didn't come all at once.

Sometimes, I had no answers at all. There were times when I would just be - looking out a window, watching a television show, reading a book, or just gazing at a picture - and thoughts of possibly not being here to share in my sons' graduations, my daughter's life with my grandsons, or my older sons having children without me would flood my mind. How was I going to look into my husband's eyes and think of him being here without me? How could I even bear the thought of him being with someone else? Damn it! How on earth am I going to get through this?

I remember I started seeing all of this pink stuff, and people suggested I should go to a support group. Inside my denial, I thought, "If

I see the color pink again or hear one more cutesy, wootsie breast cancer slogan, I am going to puke." In the beginning, I felt like I was going crazy. It was suggested that I should talk to a counselor. I was told I needed a support system, blah, blah, blah, blah, blah.

But in the end, I knew that resilience and gratitude were the keys to finding hope amidst the chaos. My journey had just begun, and I was ready to face it with strength and grace, one step at a time.Embracing Emotional Release: How Crying Contributes to Healing, we delve into the cathartic effects of crying on healing and emotional well-being. Crying is a natural and essential part of the human experience, allowing us to express and process a wide range of emotions. When we cry, we not only release pent-up feelings but also promote self-awareness and self-acceptance, which are crucial for emotional healing. Crying serves as a valuable coping mechanism during times of stress, grief, and emotional turmoil. By releasing emotional tension, crying provides relief and helps to maintain emotional balance. Research has indicated that shedding tears can stimulate the release of oxytocin and endorphins – chemicals that reduce pain and promote feelings of well-being.

Moreover, crying aids in reducing stress by eliminating stress hormones and toxins from the body. As a result, the immune system can function more effectively, contributing to overall physical healing. Crying also lowers blood pressure and heart rate, making it an effective way to alleviate tension and promote relaxation.

For those undergoing treatment for breast cancer or other illnesses, the emotional journey can be as challenging as the physical one. Crying enables us to process and come to terms with our emotions, fostering resilience and emotional strength during difficult times. By embracing the healing power of tears, we're able to better cope with the emotional rollercoaster

that often accompanies a serious health condition.

In conclusion, crying plays a significant role in healing and emotional well-being. It serves as a natural outlet for emotional expression, enabling us to experience relief and catharsis. At this stage, tears were my best friend, literally!

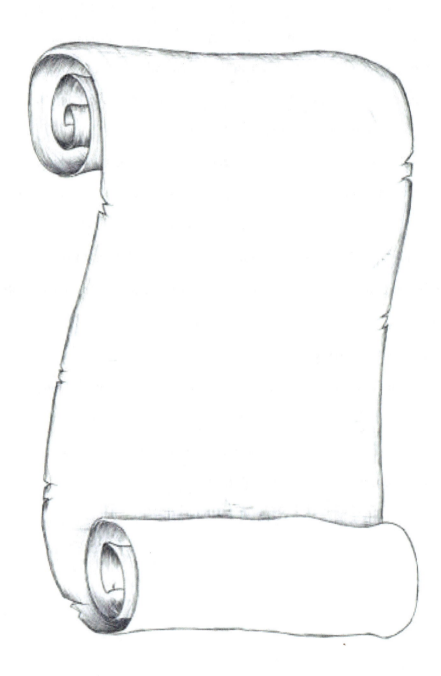

7. VOYAGE

In the tempest that is a breast cancer diagnosis, I was thrown into a churning sea of emotions, threatening to engulf me in despair. Yet, it was within these very depths that I found solace, connection, and triumph.

As the gales of fear and uncertainty whipped around me, I realized I could not traverse these waters alone. I sought the guidance of a professional therapist, whose wisdom and support became my anchor. Their presence steadied me amidst the chaos, a safe haven where I could brave the tempest of my emotions.

I embarked on an emotional voyage, daring to ride the waves of healing. To mend my soul, I allowed myself to be swept away by the full spectrum of emotions birthed by my diagnosis. I embraced fear, anger, and sadness, rather than stifling their voices. Each emotion coursed through me like a tide, a vital current in the river of my healing journey. In the eye of the storm, I found camaraderie among other breast cancer survivors. Our connection was akin to a fleet of ships, each battling the same raging seas. We shared our stories and offered support, forging unbreakable bonds that carried us through the tempest.

Together, we found solace in a lighthouse of shared experience, guiding us towards hope and healing. These triumphs, both grand and humble, became markers of my resilience and determination. Each one a testament that I could overcome any challenge life dared to present, invigorating my spirit as I journeyed towards the haven of healing.

AFFIRM

1. I AM healing and becoming stronger every day.

2. I AM surrounded by love and support from my friends and family.

3. I AM resilient and capable of overcoming any challenges.

4. I AM nourishing my body with healthy foods and positive thoughts.

5. I AM attracting health, vitality, and well-being into my life.

6. I AM embracing my body's natural ability to heal and regenerate.

7. I AM grateful for the strength and courage I have to face this journey.

8. I AM focusing on the present moment and letting go of any worries or fears.

9. I AM deserving of health, happiness, and a vibrant life.

10. I AM a powerful warrior who will triumph over cancer.

11. I AM releasing all negativity and embracing positivity and love.

12. I AM confident in my medical team and the treatment plan we have chosen.

13. I AM visualizing my body healing and becoming cancer-free.

14. I AM surrounded by healing energy and light.

15. I AM taking each day as an opportunity to grow, learn, and heal.

Remember to repeat these affirmations daily, either out loud or silently to yourself, and to truly

believe in their power. They can help to create a positive mindset, which can contribute to overall

well-being and support the healing process.

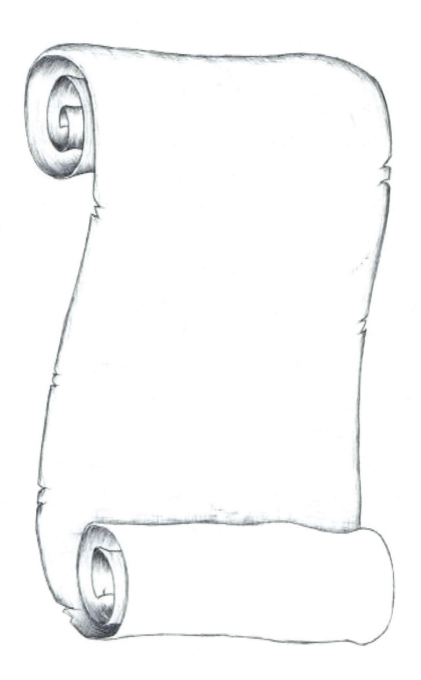

8. PHOENIX

I recall shouting to the heavens, questioning why I was chosen to face this tribulation. At that moment, I couldn't have felt further from the path of righteousness. "God, are you listening?" My thoughts raced. Initially, all I craved was to drown my sorrows in alcohol. A drink was all I needed. My mind insisted on maintaining my daily routine, clinging to any semblance of normalcy. Thus, I resolved to proceed with my scheduled manicure, hoping it could provide the solace I so desperately sought. "Perhaps this is the answer?" I wondered. My car screeched to a halt, akin to a dramatic scene from an old Batman film where justice was fiercely served. There I was, parked right in front of a liquor store, and in no time, I found myself seated in the nail salon. Tears cascaded down my cheeks as I submerged one hand into the liquid bowl, while the other frantically searched my purse for the tiny bottles of clear Bacardi Rum. Within five minutes, all six bottles were emptied, the alcohol coursing through my veins as tears flowed unabated.

The young woman attending to my nails looked bewildered. I believe she suspected my actions but hesitated to confront me. Instead, she summoned her mother, the salon's owner, who typically did my nails. They exchanged seats, and the mother initiated casual conversation with me, her eyes scrutinizing me, attempting to decipher the contents of my purse.

Her inquiries grew more poignant as she tried to comprehend the turmoil engulfing one of her most faithful clients. As I shared the devastating news of my first cancer diagnosis, she too was rendered speechless, motionless, and sorrowful, mirroring my own reactions upon hearing the dreadful news. She didn't dare ask me to cease drinking in the salon; rather, she kindly offered me a coke, likely assuming my throat had been scorched by now. But if it was, I didn't feel a thing. For an ephemeral moment, she coaxed a smile onto my face. In defiance of the life-altering revelation, I selected the most ostentatious nail color I could find. Definitely, NOT PINK! "Why me, Lord? No more," I whispered to myself. That day, the fire within me was ignited, fueling a determination to rise from the ashes of despair and face my battle with unwavering grit.

"I've never felt a pain that didn't bear a blessing."
~Gene Knudson Hoffman

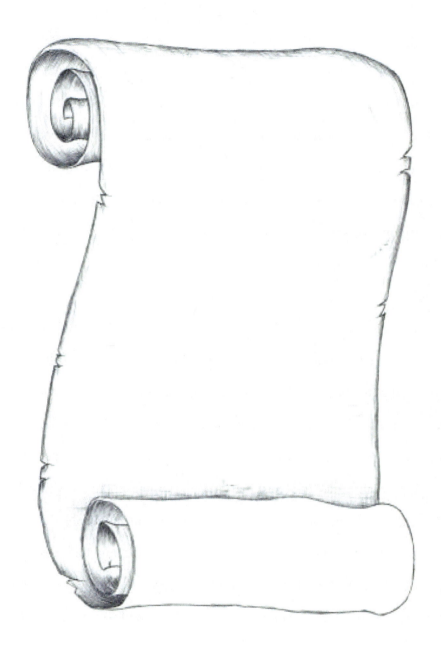

9. REKINDLED

There I was, struggling to accept the fact that I would not be the perfect Christian with an inspiring testimony for others to admire. You know, the kind of testimony that's shared at church where someone recounts how their test transformed into a testimony. They speak of the scriptures that allowed them to stand tall, to claim their healing by relying on God's promises, and to bring forth what seemed impossible. They testify about invoking the power of healing and witnessing it come to life.

I apologize if I've alienated every believer out there. I know this isn't the way I was raised to view God's promises, nor how I truly believed in the power of His word and the efficacy of what I considered to be the ultimate truth. I'm talking about the engrafted word that becomes flesh, that is created through the utterance of a word and faith as small as a mustard seed. Until that fateful moment in the doctor's office, that's what I, Lolita Arnez Jackson, held as my unshakable truth.

I, Lolita Arnez, would lay hands on the sick, and they would recover. I, Lolita Arnez, would send forth the word, and healing would follow. I, Lolita Arnez, would minister to the homeless, the sick and shut-in, and those lost souls seeking their way. I would be the first to proclaim, "God, I'll go. Test me, Lord. Use me, let me make you proud. Place me in the lion's den, try me with the trials of Job. I'll never deny you like Peter, not once and certainly not thrice."

The reality didn't unfold as I'd imagined, but ironically, it had striking similarities. The devil came for me as he did for Job, seeking my life. But God said no, and the rest of the story comprises the events unfolding between the devil's request (the diagnosis) and the eventual restoration.

My life was crumbling, and I couldn't stop it. I had been shoved off a cliff, suspended in midair, plummeting downward without a parachute, uncertain of what awaited me at the bottom. Would it be water? If so, would it be scorching hot, ice-cold, or would there be nothing at all, causing me to land face-first and meet my untimely end? I didn't know. I couldn't find my faith. It had abandoned me.

"I've never felt a pain that didn't bear a blessing." In the midst of my raw, unfiltered emotions, I'd come to discover the strength that resided within me. My faith, once shattered, would rekindle and forge an even more resilient spirit.

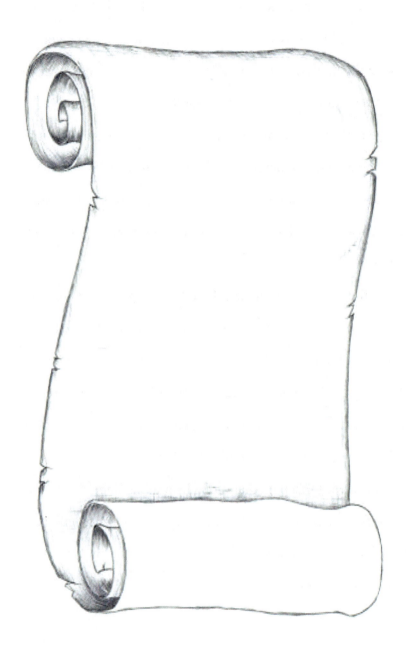

10. RESILIENCE

A few days have passed, and I've noticed that the first thing I do every morning is reach for the sheets, bunch them between my fingers, and think, "Oh my God, I'm still alive." There isn't a day that goes by that I don't wake up and say, "Thank you, Lord, for blessing me with another day." (To this day!)

Tears still flow, at times, I start crying and laughing simultaneously. I have a saying: the devil only gets fifteen minutes of my time a day. I won't give any more than that; I can't afford to give negativity that much time.

Unsure of what to do, I knew that I was still in shock and that being given a diagnosis like that would require me to find strength from somewhere other than myself just to get out of bed each day. What came next, I don't think any woman in the world could ever prepare herself for, nor should she have to. But according to statistics, millions of women have had to face the breast cancer demon and make life-altering decisions daily. If I had an enemy, I wouldn't wish what I was about to experience on her.

Amid my head spinning, tears flowing, and telephone calls coming one after the other,I still needed to go back to the doctor's office and see what all of this meant.

I was told I needed to see an oncologist and a surgeon. My next appointment was with a female breast surgeon. I didn't understand why I needed to see a breast surgeon. I was on autopilot, so I just kept moving, not even realizing that the doctor I was going to see next was the surgeon.

I walked into the office, and there were women sitting in the waiting area, looking unassuming. No one made eye contact.

"Mrs. Jackson, the doctor will see you now."

"Hello, Mrs. Jackson," said the doctor.

I thought this would be easy. I'd go in, and she'd make me feel better. But feeling better was far from what I experienced. She had a copy of my mammogram, biopsy report, and MRI.

She had also spoken with the radiologist. As she began drawing a diagram on a sheet of paper, she explained my breast, the tumor, and the fact that it was primarily inside the milk duct. We wouldn't know for sure whether the cancer had spread until they removed lymph nodes during surgery.

She believed that removing my entire breast would be the best solution due to the tumor's size. It felt like a Batman scene again with sound effects: "ERRK, SCREECH, BAM, POW, BANG!" I didn't really realize who this lady doctor was until she started telling me that because I had a tumor measuring 9½ centimeters in length and 3 inches in width and depth, they would have to remove my breasts. The entire experience was matter-of-fact, cold, and downright unbelievable. I sat there, amazed and unable to believe what she was saying. Remove, take off—I sat there, thinking, how do I get off this hamster wheel? How do I make it all stop? And then came the tears, more tears from hell and back. I had to decide whether to have surgery on my left breast, with the possibility of reconstruction or not. I could choose not to have reconstruction at all, remove both breasts at the same time and have a bilateral mastectomy because there was a possibility of cancer appearing in the right breast, although there were no indications that it would. To make a better-informed decision about the bilateral mastectomy, it was suggested that I have a genetic test to determine if I were predisposed to breast cancer genetically, that would help with the decision of removing one or both breasts at the same time (bilateral) or I could just remove one completely.

Alternatively, I could consider a lumpectomy, where they remove the tumor and some surrounding tissue but leave the breast. However, because the tumor is so large, that's not a strong recommendation; it's just an option that we must tell you about, Lolita, so that we make sure you're armed and fully equipped with all the information.

"Whew! Really? What about shrinking the tumor first, yes or no?"

"No, Lolita!"

Shrinking the tumor was not an option for me.

Now, I'm sitting there with the doctor and I have a million questions in my head, but they're not all coming out of my mouth. I have all the questions that family and friends wanted me to ask, the questions I want to ask, and then there's that list of questions that you don't even know how to ask. With a lumpectomy, I'd walk away from surgery with my breast still on my chest instead of the alternative. For example, hindsight is 20/20. What I didn't know to ask at the time was, "How likely is it that the images from the MRI are much larger than they really are?"

What I know now is that if the MRI shows a tumor of 9 ½ centimeters in length and another 3 inches in width and depth, more than likely the tumor is about half that size in length and width. With margins measuring half the size, it would produce a much smaller tumor, and with a much smaller tumor, I'd be looking at a better chance of a successful lumpectomy versus a full mastectomy.

I had genetic testing; I was not predisposed to breast cancer. The choice was made. I made my decision, feeling armed with the best information from the best medical professionals and my very own genetic testing. To ease some of my clear anxiety about the removal of my left breast, the surgeon told me to look at it this way, Lolita, "Your breasts are not an essential body part!" Meaning, I don't need my breast for life or death!

It's not like having a lung removed or a kidney or, for that matter, a limb. It's just a breast. "I do this every day; it's just another body part!" Well, I'll be damned, is this woman serious? She was. That was her attitude when I walked in, and while I was sitting there trying to process the rest of what she had to say, I knew that I was going to seek another professional opinion.

Now, let me just say this: if you are going to seek a second opinion, you might not want to tell the doctor you're having a consultation with that you're going to seek the opinion of someone else. I've found that they don't take kindly to that. I guess there was good news out of all of this: I could look forward to having breast reconstruction. "It's an option and a positive thing for you, Lolita. Don't worry, be happy. Women do it every day," said the female doctor, the lady surgeon. I do remember that I started thinking, "I get to have a brand new breast, one that no kids have sucked on, one that sits up high and not down low." The female doctor, the lady surgeon, started sounding better and better by the minute. She was offering me a little ray of hope; some sunshine was coming through the window. But now, I'm feeling like crazy lady Lolita. I walked out of that doctor's office, saying, "I need a second opinion. I received my second opinion and left that doctor's office thinking, "I need a third opinion." After getting my third opinion, I found myself saying, "I need a fourth opinion." Ultimately, all paths lead back to the advice of the first surgeon and oncologist.

I must admit, going from one doctor's office to another is incredibly tedious, but it's also essential for peace of mind. Seeking multiple professional opinions allows you to gather enough information to make an informed decision.

I call this process "fact-finding." During the discovery phase, you'll find that the wealth of information available can be overwhelming. Having someone by your side to take detailed notes and keep you organized is invaluable.

As the patient, your mind may still be reeling from the initial diagnosis, while your body rushes to gather the best professional advice to make informed decisions about life-altering surgeries or treatments.

If possible, it's crucial to have an advocate, someone to help you navigate the process after being diagnosed with breast cancer or any other form of cancer.

For me, I didn't stop at one doctor's opinion; I sought advice from four different doctors before deciding to undergo a mastectomy. I thought I had a solid plan until my third doctor suggested chemotherapy and radiation.

Suddenly, everything came screeching to a halt, again.

Up until that point, no one had mentioned chemotherapy or radiation.

I was utterly confused. I began asking all my doctors, "If I were your wife, mother, or daughter, what would you recommend for me?"

All of them assured me that they were suggesting the same course of action they would recommend for their own family members. Hearing this did provide some comfort. However, when the third doctor brought up chemotherapy and radiation, I knew I needed another opinion to make sense of it all. Let me clarify: I can't say what I would recommend to anyone else. I was overwhelmed with information, and it felt like there were too many cooks in the kitchen. I needed another opinion to either confirm or debunk the new suggestion of chemo and radiation. Up until that point, I had been feeling relatively positive about my cancer diagnosis, if that's even possible. I thought I was dodging a bullet—no chemo, no radiation. I had cancer, but I wasn't going to lose my hair. I felt special, blessed, and protected by a higher power. But then, reality hit. A doctor was now telling me not only did I need chemo, but also radiation. It was a whirlwind of emotions and confusion, a far cry from the sense of relief I had felt just moments before.

AFFIRM

My body is strong and capable of healing itself.

I trust my body's ability to fight cancer and restore balance.

I am surrounded by loving and supportive people who want to see me heal.

My cancer is a temporary challenge that I am capable of overcoming.

I am resilient and will not let cancer define me.

I am grateful for the medical treatments and support that are helping me heal.

I am worthy of health and happiness, and I will do everything in my power to achieve it.

I am sending love and positivity to every cell in my body.

I am strong and capable of handling any obstacle that comes my way.

I trust in the healing power of nature and will nourish my body with healthy foods.

I choose to focus on the positive aspects of my life, rather than dwelling on the negative.

My body is responding well to treatment, and I am getting stronger every day.

I am grateful for the opportunity to learn and grow from this experience.

I am surrounded by positivity and light, which helps me stay motivated and hopeful.

I am grateful for the love and support of my family and friends, who help me stay strong.

I am worthy of a happy, healthy, and cancer-free life.

I choose to focus on the present moment and let go of worries about the future.

My body is working hard to heal, and I am doing everything in my power to support it.

I trust that the universe is conspiring in my favor, and everything will work out for the best.

I am grateful for every day I get to spend with my loved ones, and I will cherish every moment.

"Change something, something will change."

~Lolita Jackson

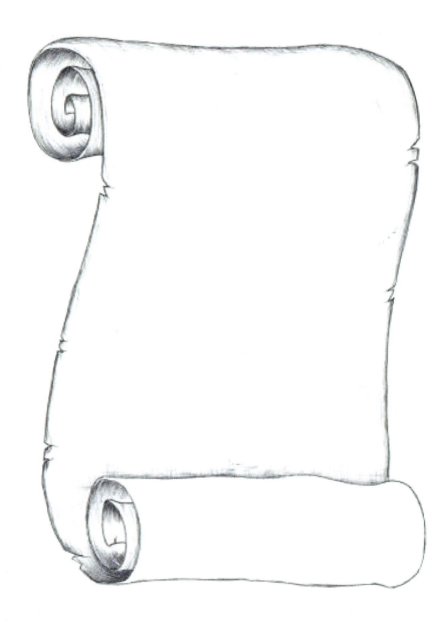

11. HEALED

Cry, cry baby… The tears will not cease, even after giving the devil his fifteen minutes. They flow like Niagara Falls, unrelenting and unstoppable. Deciding to remove my breast was a decision fraught with agony, akin to a man pondering the removal of his penis or testicles. Yet, astonishingly, many people hold cavalier attitudes about it. I couldn't believe the insensitive words spewing from their mouths, comments no woman facing my decision should ever hear. I was called shallow for my agonizing deliberation and told to "find some straws at the drug store and suck it up!" Unbelievable! Even a potential surgeon, a woman, dismissed it as a body part of insignificance.

Upon consulting a fourth doctor, I opted out of chemo and radiation, choosing mastectomy over lumpectomy. Understanding breast cancer and mastectomy is crucial. A disease affecting both men and women, breast cancer is more common in women. Mastectomy, a surgical procedure removing one or both breasts, is a typical treatment. Though often effective, it carries significant emotional and psychological ramifications.

Losing a breast to mastectomy can be overwhelmingly emotional

74

and traumatic. Women may feel grief, sadness, and fear, struggling to accept their altered appearance. The procedure can result in scarring, changes in breast shape, and altered nipple sensation. Coping with these changes demands time and support from loved ones.

Many women who have undergone mastectomy experience fear and anxiety about cancer recurrence. We may worry about losing our other breast and feel anxious about follow-up appointments and screenings.

Grieving and mourning are natural responses to the profound loss of a breast. Seeking support from loved ones and healthcare professionals is essential. Mastectomy can impact a woman's self-esteem and body image, making them feel less feminine or attractive. Focusing on self-care and rebuilding self-esteem is crucial. Mastectomy can also affect a woman's relationships and intimacy. Women may worry about their partners' perceptions and struggle with insecurity and shame. Open communication with partners and support from healthcare professionals are key. While mastectomy is a challenging and emotional experience, focusing on moving forward and adapting to a new reality is crucial. With time, support, and self-care, many women find peace and acceptance after mastectomy. That being said, for me it wasn't as black and white as these pages…

"Be brave, good things will happen."

~Naszier Paschal

"Don't react to other people's actions."

~Stephen Jackson

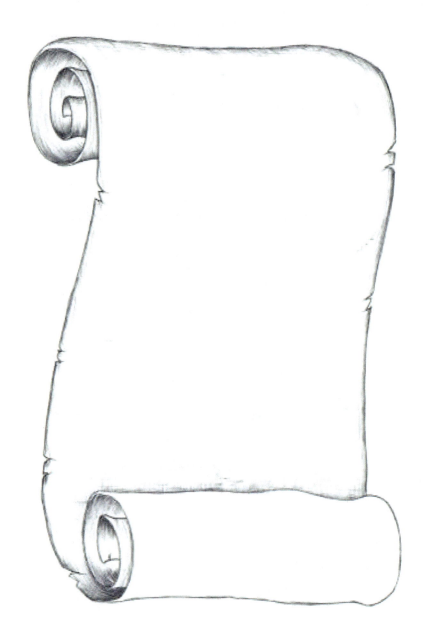

12. FEARLESS

I have yet to find a book, article, or person who genuinely delves into the experience of having a mastectomy and the pain we feel when faced with the decision to remove our breasts. It may ultimately come down to choice, but just because a doctor recommends it and your life depends on it, doesn't mean you'll choose to go through with it. Some women cannot, for various reasons, go through with the doctor's recommendation, and live with their choice, whether it leads to a positive or negative outcome.

Dealing with a breast cancer diagnosis can be overwhelming, and often the only solace is sleep. When I wasn't sleeping, I was bombarded with thoughts and emotions that are difficult to process. I didn't want to face these thoughts, but eventually, I had to confront the boogeyman in my head. The fear that no woman ever wants to face was staring me down.

At first, I had fleeting thoughts like, "What will my husband do?" "Will he still love me without my breasts?" "How will this affect our sex life?" These thoughts would come and go, but as time went on, they became more persistent, and I could no longer dismiss them.

I discovered stories of women who couldn't face the removal of their breasts and those who did. The fear of their husbands looking at them differently and the changes to their bodies and appearances was too much to bear for some, leading them to gamble with their lives. I wanted assurance that my husband would still love me, that he would be the kind of man who would say that my scar is beautiful because it represents the saving of my life.

The promise of reconstruction made my decision palatable. But the thought of losing my breast was still excruciating, and I often had to compare it to a man losing his penis to help them understand the devastation I felt.

Deciding to have a mastectomy and remove my breast involved several factors. As a married woman, my first concern was how my husband would feel about it? That was a huge factor in trying to figure out what I was going to do and what he was going to do? Everyone had an opinion, but in the end, it was my decision to make.

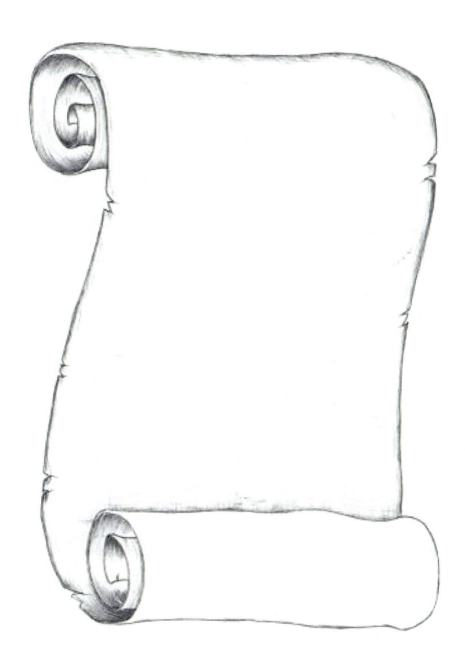

13. MASTECTOMY

I have yet to find a book, article, or person who genuinely discusses the experience of having a mastectomy and the pain associated with making the decision to have our breasts removed. I say it comes down to choice since, ultimately, it is up to us whether to follow the doctor's recommendation, even when our very lives depend on it. Some women, though few and far between, cannot or will not go through with the procedure for various reasons, living with the consequences of their choice, be they good, bad, or indifferent.

After a breast cancer diagnosis, there's so much to deal with that the only thing that seems to help with the runaway thoughts is sleep. When I'm not sleeping, these feelings, emotions, and thoughts are present. I didn't want to deal with them because when they first arose, they were merely fleeting thoughts that I would quickly dismiss. But now, I must confront these boogeyman thoughts, the ones no woman ever wants to face. The devil that no woman wants to meet lies within Pandora's Box – a box I didn't even know existed.

Upon being diagnosed with breast cancer, I'd periodically be tormented by thoughts like, "What will my husband do?" "Will he still love me without my breasts?" "Will he still look at me the same?" "How will this affect our sex life?" "Can I just have a lumpectomy even if I need a mastectomy?" "What will he do when another woman with breasts comes into our presence?" "Will he look at her chest?" "How will I handle that situation?" "Will I envy women who have breasts?" "Will I now scrutinize every woman with breasts?" "What if I don't do anything and just take my chances because I don't want things to change in the bedroom with us?" Keeping these awful thoughts in my head and spirit would have driven me insane.

Then there were the conversations and Google searches that exposed me to women who couldn't or didn't face the removal of their breasts, as well as those who did. The thoughts of their husbands and now wives, yes you heard me, now women with women have the same feelings and emotions dealing with their significant others as I had with my husband, looking at them differently and the changes that would take place with their bodies and appearances were too much to bear. As a result, some chose to take their chances with their lives and opted not to remove their breasts, leading to their demise for some. I wanted to be assured that my husband would still love me. I wanted him to be that doting, loving husband you hear stories about—the one who tells his wife, recently diagnosed with breast cancer, that he doesn't care about her breasts. The husband who says, "Your scar is beautiful because it represents the saving of your life!" I wanted that husband, that man, so I could move forward with certainty that even if I underwent a mastectomy, everything would be alright in our lives because my marriage was built on unconditional love.

I needed to hear that from my husband. I needed him to say it without me having to ask him. I needed him to take me in his arms and say, "Lolita, I love you to the moon and back." Well, now, it didn't happen like that for me. It kind of did, sort of, but not really. The first diagnosis was a little better than the second. My husband told me how much he loved me. He professed his love for me, maybe not in the way I envisioned it, but he did say it, and he did show it, and for that, I'm eternally grateful. Now, there were other extenuating circumstances that may have added some weight and may have been a factor. There was the promise of new breasts, which made the decision to remove my breasts a bit easier for both of us.

Now, that's woman to man; then there's the woman to woman talks, feelings, looks, stares, general questions, and the whole gamut of "here we go!"

There are several extenuating factors that play out in the decision-making process of having a mastectomy and the removal of your breasts. For me, as a married woman, my first thought was: what was my husband going to think or do? That's HUGE, trying to figure out what I was going to do. What was he going to do? Trust me, I heard it all from everyone else who didn't have to make MY decision about what I could, should, or what they would do, right? For some, removing the breasts isn't that big of a deal. For me, it was, partly because I knew that my husband LOVED my breasts. My breasts were a significant part of OUR enjoyment! Plain and simple, this man was all over them, in every way he could think of, and to our delight, I let him have it all. We were married, I was his little Pam Grier, and my body and breasts were just like hers back in the day. My breasts were the CENTER of attention and the "Main Attraction" ALL the time in our lives together.

I read a book by Brian Tracy called 'Eat that Frog,' and the premise of the book is when it comes to daily tasks, instead of putting off the hardest, most difficult, challenging task of your day until last, tackle it first! Eat the frog first and get it out of the way early in the day so that the rest of your tasks for the remainder of the day will be a piece of cake.

That brings me to my frog. In order for me to be true to myself, my readers, and the lemons I have been served during my experience with breast cancer, I'm compelled to lay it ALL out and speak to the REAL fears, concerns, and experiences that I had and to some that other women have had to deal with breast cancer and everything that comes with it.

Will my husband notice the breasts more now that I don't have them? Is it fair to him to be married to me forever and expect him never to touch another pair of breasts again just because I don't have my breasts? How will I deal with the women who will come around and deliberately flaunt their breasts in my face and my husband's because they now know that they have something that I don't have? How will I know the difference? Are ALL women suspect now? Am I overthinking this? Are my concerns legitimate, or am I really about to be insecure? What am I going to do if my husband turns out to be the guy who says he can't live without touching breasts forever? What if my husband is not the guy who tells his wife, 'I don't give a damn about your breasts; all I care about is you, Lolita'? What if my husband turns out to be the guy who never touches me again because he can't bear the sight of my body now that it is marred and disfigured? What if my husband reaches out and into the arms of another woman? What if he lays his head on her chest and in her breasts and finds comfort and solace with someone else? What if my husband decides that he wants a divorce deep down in his soul, but he doesn't want to be the guy that everyone will look at as the guy who left his wife because she had her breasts removed and, at the bottom line, he couldn't deal with it? What would I do if my husband never touched me again intimately for years? What if the answer to every question, fear, concern, and insecurity were that of my worst dreams and outright nightmares?"

Sometimes, I think it would have been easier to have been single going through breast cancer because I wouldn't have had to think about and deal with any of those questions and "what if" concerns and fears. I actually did think that until I spoke with a single friend who had undergone breast cancer and she was telling me about how differently her experience would've been had she been married and had someone to share it with? Wow, just wow, I thought about how the grass really isn't greener unless it's watered! I wasn't single, and I had to deal with everything that I just mentioned, and my life was turned upside down.

How did I make lemonade out of my situation? I'm making it now; daily, I add to the pitcher of life. My husband has been the guy that I was once starting to write a book about, describing how wonderful he is. I still might do that, stay tuned… . I mean, I could look up the book/journal and read you some excerpts that would make your head spin with all the passages of love and adoration that this man had for me. Every day, and I mean every day, my husband would come home and tell me how beautiful I was. He would tell me how much he loved me, and he would come home and ask me to show him how to love me. This man professed his undying love for me forever and a day! I would get flowers just because, and plants—he knew that I loved plants, so he was always bringing me plants....

The surgery went well. Awakening in the recovery room, I found my left breast gone. Though the doctor mentioned a JP tube sticking out of my chest wall to collect fluid, I hadn't fully grasped its reality. This Jackson-Pratt Tube, a plastic ball attached to a 24-inch tube, collected fluids from my breast. I emptied the tube daily, charting the fluid measurements until I reached less than 20 cc in a 24-hour period.

In addition to the mastectomy, I chose breast reconstruction. The breast surgeon left some skin, allowing the plastic surgeon to insert a device to be gradually filled with fluid. Once it reached the desired size, I'd undergo another surgery to replace the device with an implant.

Now, it's here, at this point in the story where things shifted, cosmically the earth was turning on its axis and I was in auto-pilot.

All of the story above is actual/factual, but life can be funny and peculiar, you'll think that someone must be following you around with a hidden camera because if you think the above story is something, wait until I tell you about the RECONSTRUCTION NIGHTMARES! Which, by the way will lead into book two simply because there were so many surgeries due to complication after complication that by the time I even had a full reconstructed breast to look at, unbeknownst to me, I was literally dealing with the pains of Breast Cancer in my second breast on the right side…

Cliffhanger ...

Reconstruction, I've decided to go into details about my experiences with reconstruction as the opening chapter to book two of this three part trilogy of my experiences with being diagnosed with Breast Cancer, not once, not twice but three times...

My reasons, I have had countless surgeries and complications that have been insurmountable.

Stay tuned, coming soon!

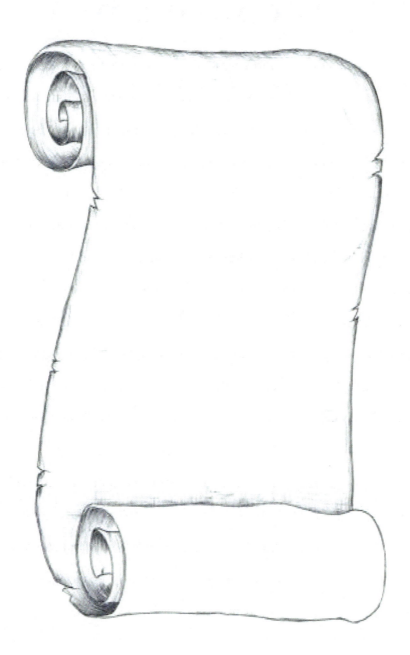

14. COMPASSION

The deluge of support cascaded from all corners of life. Cards, meals, phone calls, and the time and energy people invested in me were truly remarkable. This journey cultivated my spiritual growth. Before the diagnosis, I was deeply religious, steadfast in my beliefs about God and Jesus Christ. I thought my way was the only way. Raised in such an environment, I held all the answers. If you belonged to another faith - Mormon, Jehovah's Witness, Muslim, Catholic, practiced Buddhism, or anything contrary to COGIC - I would have fervently prayed with and for you, invoking the blood of Jesus, casting out demons, laying hands, and guiding you to the cross, as I believed you were lost with an unrepentant heart and soul. I eagerly awaited the knock on the door, ready to bring CHURCH into my home. Little did I know, God had different plans for me.

One of my many transformative moments came from individuals of different faiths and beliefs, and some who didn't adhere to any formal religion. They were just kind-hearted people who loved and cared for me and my family. They took the time to prepare meals, ensuring my son had a hot meal when he returned from school. Friends came to do my hair or sent pizza delivery when they couldn't visit. A friend consistently sent me cards of encouragement, each one a blessing. Another friend even gifted my husband a car - yes, a car! People called to tell me they were praying for me, and I couldn't get enough of it. I added my name to every prayer list I could find, reaching out to every station, ministry, and person who appeared to have a direct line to God, asking them to stand in the gap with me and for me in prayer.

In search of answers and support, I pursued every avenue necessary, embracing the wings of compassion that surrounded me.

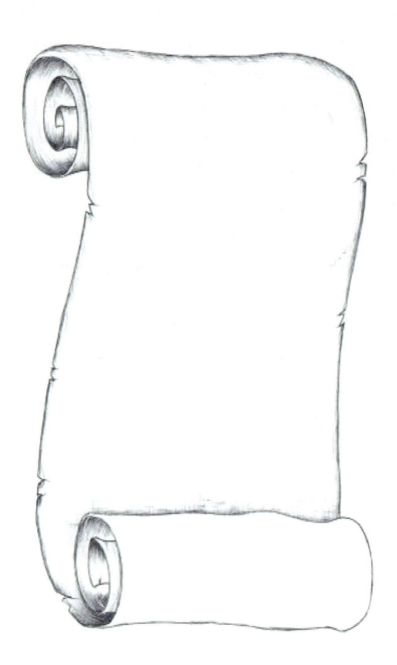

15. ALLO/NATURO

Allopathy: The method of treating disease by the use of agents that produce effects different from those of the disease being treated.

Naturopathy: A method of treating a disease that employs no surgery or synthetic drugs but uses fasting, special diets, massages, etc., to assist the natural healing processes.

When faced with treating breast cancer, I found myself in the midst of a bewildering labyrinth. Unaware of the myriad treatment options available, I had never been diagnosed with the disease, nor had I personally spent time with or witnessed anyone dealing with breast cancer and its multifaceted aspects.

Many people prefer a hands-on approach to their care and treatment. I, however, wished I had a patient care representative to help me organize, document, and advocate for me, given my lack of knowledge about the disease, treatments, and options. The sheer enormity of being diagnosed with the "C" word was, for me and many others, overwhelming. Cancer is not a diagnosis the average person can easily cope with.

I believe I navigated the maze and onslaught of information reasonably well. Still, I can't help but think about the unnecessary stress caused by my ignorance of the disease and the struggle to process and assimilate the information, ultimately leading to the right treatment, recovery, healing, and survivorship.

I quickly learned that a combination of allopathic and naturopathic treatments would be advantageous for me. The allopathic approach is the conventional mainstream method, based on years of clinical trials, studies, science, research, and development. In contrast, naturopathy offered a holistic approach to my care and treatment, encompassing mind, body, spirit, nutrition, and soul therapies. As a spiritually astute person, I knew I would intertwine both methods, leading to some of the most uplifting and invigorating experiences of my life.

I surrounded myself with an incredible team, a compassionate assembly of doctors, nurses, therapists, counselors, coaches, nutritionists, pharmacists, spiritual advisors, leaders, prayer partners, prayer warriors, support group team members, friends, family, and my dog, Carmello. I allowed myself to truly experience going beyond the veil, sitting by God's throne, and worshiping in spirit and truth. By embracing the omniscient presence of God's spirit, I transformed and evolved, fostering growth and healing in my mind, soul, and body. I opened myself to various healing methods, much like Jesus did in the Bible. His unconventional methods, such as creating mud from dirt to open blinded eyes, demonstrated his saving, healing grace of mercy and forgiveness. Inspired by his example, I looked beyond the confines of religion and conformity, discovering God's spirit of grace, mercy, forgiveness, and healing in unconventional ways.

I now recognize the truth in the saying that I might not have known God if God had been right in front of me almost 16 years ago because I was so religious that I was no earthly good. I am honored and profoundly grateful for the opportunity that fostered growth within me.

I experienced acupuncture, reiki energy cleansing, meditation, and prayer. I recited healing mantras, divine words revealed to me by God's spirit. I saw firsthand how prayer works in the spiritual realm. Nutritionally, I regularly consumed juices made from whole, clean, organic produce. I listened to and created tapes with my personal mantras of healing and inspiration, which I consistently spoke into my spirit and existence. I learned to call upon those things that were not as if they were, becoming a pillar of strength and resilience. I remember countless instances when I visited my oncologist's office, had a blood draw, and

My white blood count would sometimes be low, prompting the doctor to consider prescribing medication. However, there were instances when it was so low that he couldn't provide the prescription he intended to give me. In those situations, I would ask him for a couple of days to improve my blood count. Sure enough, when I returned, my numbers would be remarkable, leaving him unsure about what to do next. Naturally, I would lean toward not taking any medication.

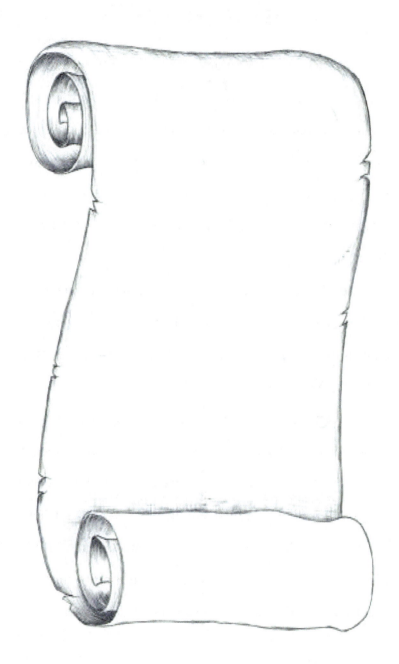

16. SERENDIPITY

I used to manage a Christian Book Store, and I loved to read. I would read anything and everything that piqued my curiosity. I purchased a book about juicing and how juicing could cleanse people with cancer. At the time, I bought the book because A) I liked to read, and B) it had great recipes for juicing, which I enjoyed. Little did I know that three years later, I would need this book to cleanse my body of cancer.

Let me tell you how amazing the Universe, faith, and belief can be. I pulled the book out, intending to read it from cover to cover and follow all its advice. I didn't get past the first few pages before learning that the healing center and retreat location mentioned in the book were in Washington State. Intrigued, I looked up the center's number and called. To my surprise, the man who answered the phone was the co-author of the book and the owner of the wellness center. During our conversation, I·learned that the other co-author, Cherie, lived in my area literally about a mile away down the hill.

I found her number and nervously called her, she answered the phone, tears streaming down my face. I introduced myself and explained my recent cancer diagnosis. She kindly offered to help me, mentioning a consultation fee of thirty-nine ninety-five. I initially thought there's no way I can afford $3,995, but she clarified it was only $39.95. Relieved,

that $39.95 has paid for itself a million times over. Cherie, the kind and warm-hearted lady I had spoken to, welcomed me into her home and taught me everything I needed to know about wellness, health, and nutrition. She emphasized the importance of fresh, green vegetables, and water with high pH levels. Over the years, Cherie patiently guided me, and I attended her classes, absorbing her wisdom like a child.

I am grateful for Cherie Calbom, the woman who did the work of God's extended hands. She became a dear friend, and I love her for her kindness, warmth, and guidance. I almost tripped over my feet, jumping up from the couch and scrambling to find my purse. I rattled off my card number faster than I could talk. That lady, that kind, peaceful, saintly, warm lady, talked to me for hours, inviting me to her home in downtown Edmonds. Her house was one of those mansions overlooking the water, and she was married to a priest! Can you believe it? She is amazing.

We are friends to this day. Let me tell you something else about Cherie Calbom, she would let me, or my husband, or my son come to her home and fill up the 5 gallon jugs of Kangen Water for free! Cherie was there just for me! Through each experience, she was there, water, guidance, support and all! I sat at her feet, bought all her books, I absorbed her until I began to emulate and incorporate her wisdom and knowledge into my own recovery as I started my own growth journey on the importance of juicing incorporating it into my journey to wellness!.

Thank you, Cherie! P.S. Right after I began my road to recovery after the third diagnosis, Cherie moved from Edmonds, WA still blessing people on to bigger and better visions in Arizona! (you can't tell me she wasn't there for me!) Thank you for coaching me to now be the best coach I can be…

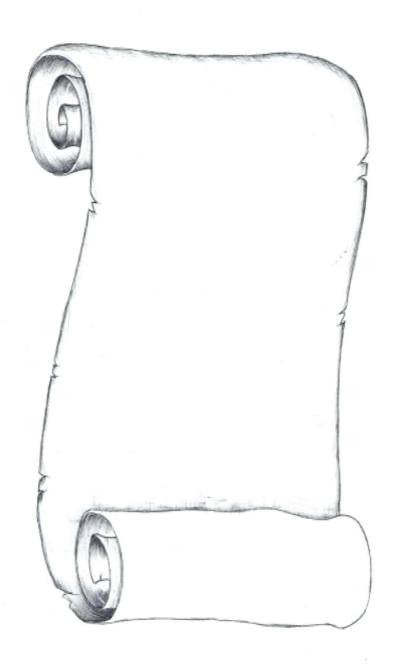

17. WATER

We've all been to a company or an office and used a water dispenser without giving it much thought. For me, that was the extent of my thoughts on water and water filters, except for a few times over the years when I rented a machine for my home and had a fancy truck deliver water to my doorstep. I even upgraded my dispenser so I could enjoy both cold and hot water.

I don't know how much you think about the water you drink daily, but I can tell you with complete honesty that before being diagnosed with breast cancer, I didn't give the water I drank much thought, other than buying bottled water from the grocery store.

Did you know that people have meetings, parties, and conferences about water? I didn't realize how important water was to the human body until my first bout with breast cancer. I wanted to do everything humanly possible to be on the right road to recovery, and I was open to any suggestions that were financially, spiritually, psychologically, emotionally, and physically reasonable. So when I was told to get a water filter and start drinking alkaline water, I asked where I could buy it and which store had it. Little did I know, I was about to be inundated with a whirlwind of information and be pulled in every direction by people, places, and things trying to get me to see, know, and buy their product, brand, and join their team.

I quickly learned everything I could about alkaline water and its health benefits. Alkaline water is rich in minerals, pH balanced, and fights acid, allowing optimal hydration within your body. Drinking alkaline ionized water helps flush out heavy metals and toxins, reducing the effects of harmful heavy metals like mercury from oxidized rust.

You may ask, "Why is all of this important to me?" It's important because our bodies can have a positive or negative ORP (Oxidation Reduction Potential) from our water. If the water in our bodies has a positive ORP, it means there's oxidation within the water and our bodies. A negative ORP measures the aqueous substance's ability to reduce oxidation, and a water ionizer can make water alkaline if it's negative.

Our pH (Potential Hydrogen) is a measurement of the acidity or alkalinity of a soluble solution. We want our bodies to have a pH that measures greater than 7, which is what alkaline water will do for you. The number 7 is considered neutral, above 7 is alkaline, and acidity is any number below 7.

Today, I know it's imperative to hydrate my body properly, and

I'm grateful to be sitting here with a sound mind and body, armed with knowledge in an area I was previously clueless in. I know there are numerous effects of pH in our bodies and not having filtered water with high alkalinity can lead to complications detrimental to my personal health.

I thought, like many others, that if it's bottled water, then it's good water, right? Wrong! Bottled water is good, but the FDA considers water bottling plants to be a low priority for inspections, and they don't have to give full disclosure on contaminants in their water or how they treat their water. The FDA checks for purification, but they do not check the pH levels of bottled water plants, allowing consumers to purchase bottled filtered tap water.

I had to do my own research on alkaline water vs. acidic water and the various water filtration systems to decide what would work best for me and why. Choosing an ionizer can be time-consuming and expensive, but it's worth every dime for your health. I buy ionized alkaline water with a pH level of 9.5 or higher.

In light of branding, marketing, sponsorship, and the sensitivities surrounding various aspects, I have chosen to refrain from mentioning specific brands, names, or companies in my book. However, if you have

105

any questions or concerns regarding names, brands, stores, and so on, please do not hesitate to reach out to me about the water I drink, the filtration ionizing system I prefer, and the lessons I've learned.

Water is vital for overall health and plays a crucial role in breast cancer recovery. It flushes toxins from the body, including those produced during cancer treatments, and helps maintain healthy hydration levels, particularly important during recovery. Dehydration can result in numerous health issues, such as fatigue, muscle weakness, and diminished immune function.

Alkaline water, with a higher pH level than regular tap water, is believed to offer health benefits, including improved hydration, enhanced digestion, and increased energy. This type of water is also thought to possess anti-inflammatory properties, which can prove advantageous for individuals recovering from breast cancer.

Alkaline water has demonstrated its benefits in breast cancer recovery in several ways. Firstly, it helps neutralize acidity in the body, crucial as cancer cells thrive in acidic environments. Furthermore, alkaline water can reduce inflammation, alleviating pain and discomfort associated with cancer treatments. Lastly, it can bolster overall hydration levels, which is essential for breast cancer recovery.

Maintaining hydration during breast cancer recovery is critical for overall health and wellness. Here are some tips for staying hydrated:

1. Drink ample water throughout the day, including alkaline water, if possible.

2. Consume water-rich foods, such as fruits and vegetables.

3. Avoid sugary or caffeinated beverages that can dehydrate the body.

4. Carry a water bottle with you at all times as a reminder to drink water.

In conclusion, hydration and alkaline water consumption are vital components of breast cancer recovery. Water aids in flushing out toxins, sustaining healthy hydration levels, and promoting overall health and wellness.

Dr. Masaru Emoto, a Japanese scientist, researcher, and author, gained widespread recognition for his groundbreaking work in water research. Born in Yokohama, Japan, in 1943, Dr. Emoto graduated from Yokohama Municipal University in 1966 and later studied at the Open International University for Alternative Medicine. In the 1990s, his interest in water's properties led him to conduct a series of experiments exploring the relationship between water and consciousness. His work has profoundly influenced holistic medicine, alternative healing, and spiritual development.

According to Dr. Masaru Emoto, water is not only a physical substance but also a carrier of information and energy. He posited that water can store and transmit emotions, thoughts, and intentions, and that these properties can be harnessed for healing and well-being. He further argued that water has a crystalline structure influenced by external stimuli, such as music, words, and images. Dr. Emoto's experiments demonstrated that positive vibrations, like love and gratitude, can positively impact water, while negative vibrations, such as fear and anger, can have detrimental effects.

One area where Dr. Emoto's work has been applied in breast cancer treatment. Water therapy for breast cancer involves exposing patients to positive vibrations through music, words, and images, aiming to stimulate the body's natural healing response. Patients are also given specially treated water infused with positive vibrations and intentions to enhance the treatment's effectiveness. This water therapy targets physical healing, emotional wellbeing, and spiritual development.

Water therapy for breast cancer offers numerous benefits. First, it can help reduce side effects from conventional cancer treatments, such as chemotherapy and radiation therapy. Second, it bolsters the immune system and encourages the body's natural healing response. Third, it can alleviate stress and anxiety, benefiting both physical and emotional wellbeing. Lastly, it promotes spiritual growth and development by connecting patients to water and consciousness healing power.

In conclusion, Dr. Masaru Emoto's work has significantly impacted water research and inspired many to investigate the relationship between water and consciousness. The water therapy treatment for breast cancer exemplifies the practical application of his theories, displaying promising results in promoting healing and wellbeing for cancer patients. As the field of holistic medicine evolves, it is likely that an increasing number of people will turn to water therapy as a natural, non-invasive, and effective treatment for various health conditions. I personally ascribe to Dr. Emoto's teachings and practices…

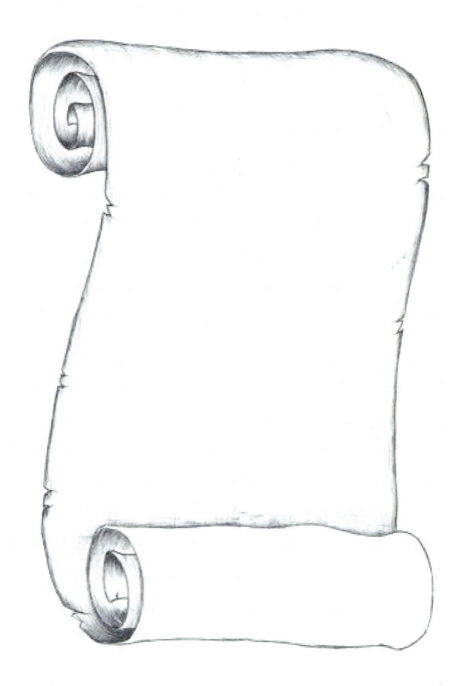

18. LEMONS

I must admit that when the idea of making lemonade out of lemons came to me, I initially saw it as a metaphor for transforming a negative experience, such as my battle with breast cancer, into something positive. At the time, I had no idea that lemons possess cancer-fighting properties and that the daily consumption of organic lemon peel and zest has been clinically shown to reduce tumors, eradicate toxins, and destroy malignant cancer cells in the body.

As I started my lemonade stand, sharing my story and how I decided to make lemonade out of the lemons life had dealt me, I also incorporated lemons into my juicing regimen. My "Lolita's Luscious Lemonade" recipe uses an entire lemon per cup, ensuring that customers get their money's worth at $5.00 a cup.

One day, while browsing the internet, I stumbled upon an article discussing the benefits of lemons in fighting cancer, and I was astonished. Tears of joy streamed down my face as I called my husband to read the article. Everything started to make sense: God had given me the idea to start making lemonade, not just as a metaphor, but also as a way to provide my body with the healing benefits of lemons.

Had I dismissed the original call to make lemonade because of the idea's absurdity, I would never have discovered the powerful potential of lemons. With every cup I serve, I am offering a cup of love with a health benefactor inside.

It amazes me to realize that my steps have been ordered and that God has a master plan for my life. When I first started selling lemonade, I worried about buying too many lemons, but I learned that freezing them preserved their freshness. Moreover, I found out that using the zest of frozen lemons has additional health benefits.

Drinking lemon water daily offers numerous health benefits due to the antioxidants found in citrus fruits. Antioxidants help reduce oxidative stress in the body and neutralize acids that promote cancer cell growth. Lemons are high in magnesium, potassium, and vitamin C, and they can also boost brainpower.

After my mastectomies, some lymph nodes were removed, compromising my lymphatic system, which helps rid the body of fatty acid fluids from tissues for proper digestion. Drinking water with lemons improves lymphatic system functionality, allowing for better fluid flow.

Lemons possess anti-inflammatory diuretic properties that aid digestion and hydration, flush out toxins, and reduce pain from swollen joints. Lemons offer many other benefits as well. They can help whiten teeth, clear up skin, and alleviate swelling and pain from bee stings and sunburns.

Lemons have gained attention in recent years for their potential role in breast cancer healing, especially the benefits of lemon zest.

Packed with essential vitamins and minerals, lemons support overall health. They are a great source of vitamin C, an antioxidant that protects cells from damage, and contain folate, potassium, and fiber, all crucial for maintaining good health.

Research has shown that lemons contain compounds that may help prevent the growth and spread of cancer cells. Limonene, a compound found in lemon zest, has demonstrated anti-cancer properties and may help prevent the development of breast cancer. Lemons are known for their alkalizing properties, which can help balance the pH levels in the body. An alkaline environment may help prevent cancer growth, as cancer cells tend to thrive in an acidic environment.

The health benefits of lemons and their zest for breast cancer healing can be attributed to several factors:

1. Antioxidant properties: Lemons are rich in antioxidants,

including vitamin C and flavonoids. These antioxidants help neutralize free radicals in the body, which can cause cellular damage and contribute to the development of cancer. By reducing oxidative stress, lemons may help protect against the initiation and progression of breast cancer.

2. Anti-inflammatory effects: Chronic inflammation has been linked to an increased risk of various types of cancer, including breast cancer. Lemons contain anti-inflammatory compounds that may help reduce inflammation in the body, potentially lowering the risk of breast cancer development.

3. Induction of apoptosis: Apoptosis is a natural process in which damaged or abnormal cells are eliminated from the body. Research has shown that certain compounds in lemons, such as limonene, can induce apoptosis in cancer cells, which may help slow down the growth and spread of breast cancer.

4. Inhibition of angiogenesis: Angiogenesis is the formation of new blood vessels, which is essential for tumor growth and metastasis. Some studies have suggested that lemon zest and its compounds may help inhibit angiogenesis, thereby reducing the growth and spread of breast cancer cells.

5. Immune system support: A strong immune system is crucial for fighting off diseases, including cancer. Lemons contain various nutrients, such as vitamin C, that can help boost the immune system and improve the body's ability to fight cancer cells.

6. Enhancement of conventional treatments: Some research indicates that lemon compounds may enhance the effectiveness of conventional breast cancer treatments like chemotherapy and radiation therapy. By increasing the sensitivity of cancer cells to these treatments, lemons may help improve treatment outcomes.

By incorporating lemons and lemon zest into your daily routine, you can take advantage of their numerous health benefits, potentially reducing the risk of developing breast cancer and supporting overall wellbeing. It is important to note, however, that lemons should be used as a complementary therapy alongside conventional cancer treatments, and not as a substitute for professional medical advice and care. ALWAYS, ALWAYS, ALWAYS, consult YOUR PHYSICIAN and get your medical advice and recommendations from your medical team not me, Lolita Jackson.

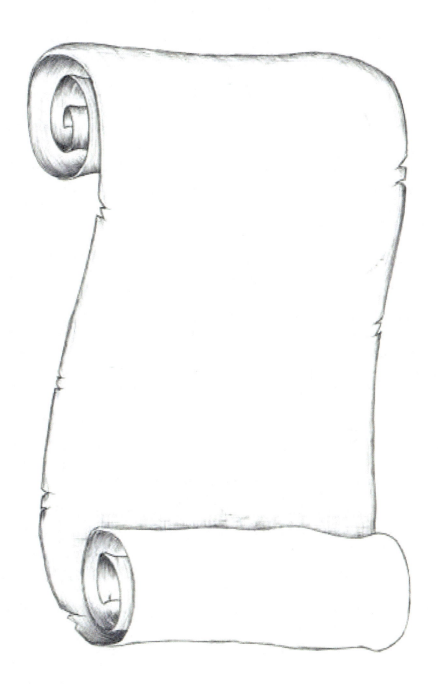

19. LAUGH

Throughout my journey with breast cancer, I discovered that laughter was an essential part of my healing process. While no doctor prescribed laughter, comedy, or fun as a remedy, I found these elements to be powerful medicine for my body, mind, and spirit. I began to embrace the therapeutic benefits of laughter as a means to cope with my disease and its challenges.

As a breast cancer patient, I had my share of dark moments. During one of these episodes, I accidentally stumbled upon the magic of laughter. Watching Steve Harvey on television, I initially resisted the urge to laugh, thinking that my world was crumbling around me. But eventually, his humor broke through my wall of despair, and I found myself laughing uncontrollably. This laughter lifted my spirits, made me forget my troubles, and brought a sense of vitality back to my body.

After this experience, I made a conscious decision to incorporate laughter into my daily routine. I sought out comedy shows, funny videos, and hilarious conversations with friends, all with the goal of filling my days with humor and joy. As I embraced laughter, I found that it began to seek me out in return, appearing in the most unexpected moments and places. Scientific studies have shown that laughter has numerous health benefits. It can boost the immune system, decrease stress hormones, and release endorphins, the body's natural feel-good chemicals. Laughter can also improve blood flow, which is essential for a healthy heart and the body's overall wellbeing.

By incorporating laughter into my daily life, I found that my mood improved, my relationships were enriched, and my overall quality of life increased. Laughter even enhanced my most intimate moments, as my husband and I shared a unique bond through our humor and joy.

In conclusion, incorporating laughter into my healing journey proved to be an essential and transformative practice. The therapeutic benefits of laughter for the body, mind, and spirit are undeniable, and I encourage others facing challenging circumstances to embrace this powerful, natural remedy. Remember, no matter the situation, laughter can be the best medicine. Here are some research findings that highlight the power of laughter as a form of medicine:

1. Boosting the immune system: A study conducted by Lee Berk and Stanley Tan at Loma Linda University in California found that laughter could increase the production of antibodies and activate

immune cells, thus strengthening the immune system (Berk, L.S., et al., 1989).

2. Reducing stress hormones: Research has shown that laughter can decrease the levels of stress hormones, such as cortisol and epinephrine, in the body (Bennett, M.P., et al., 2003). This reduction in stress hormones can help alleviate anxiety and promote relaxation.

3. Releasing endorphins: Laughter triggers the release of endorphins, the body's natural feel-good chemicals, which can contribute to a sense of well-being and even act as natural painkillers (Dunbar, R.I.M., et al., 2012).

4. Improving cardiovascular health: A study by Michael Miller and his colleagues at the University of Maryland found that laughter can increase blood flow and improve vascular function, suggesting a potential protective effect on the heart (Miller, M., et al., 2006).

5. Enhancing mental functioning: Laughter has been shown to improve cognitive function, memory, and creativity, as well as increase overall mental flexibility (Gelkopf, M., et al., 1997).

These studies and others demonstrate the significant potential of laughter as a form of medicine for both physical and mental health. By incorporating laughter into daily life, individuals can harness its healing power to support their overall well-being.

A breast diagnosis can be a challenging time for anyone. The diagnosis can be overwhelming and can cause anxiety, stress, and depression. It can be difficult to maintain a positive outlook during this time. However, laughter therapy is an effective way to reduce stress and anxiety and to promote healing. Laughter has been shown to release endorphins, which are the body's natural painkillers, and it can improve mood and immune function.

Laughter therapy has a positive effect on the brain. When we laugh, the brain releases
endorphins, which are the body's natural painkillers. Endorphins also help to reduce stress and
anxiety. Additionally, laughter has been shown to stimulate the production of neurotransmitters
like dopamine and serotonin, which can improve mood and promote feelings of well-being.
Laughter can also increase blood flow and oxygenation to the brain, which can improve
cognitive function and reduce the risk of cognitive decline.

Laughter has numerous physical health benefits. It can help to reduce blood pressure, improve cardiovascular health, and boost the immune system. Additionally, laughter therapy can reduce pain and inflammation, which can be particularly helpful for those undergoing treatment for breast diagnosis. Laughter has also been shown to improve respiratory function, reduce muscle tension, and improve digestion.

Laughter therapy can be particularly beneficial for emotional health. Laughter can reduce stress, anxiety, and depression, and it can improve mood and promote feelings of well-being.

Additionally, laughter therapy can improve social connections and reduce feelings of isolation

and loneliness. Laughter has also been shown to increase resilience and improve coping skills,

which can be particularly helpful during times of stress and adversity. Laughter therapy can be incorporated into breast diagnosis treatment in several ways. Healthcare providers can incorporate humor into their interactions with patients, and patients can participate in laughter therapy sessions with trained professionals. Overall, laughter therapy can be an effective way to promote healing and improve quality of life during breast

diagnosis treatment.

Laughter can be a powerful tool to enhance your mood and overall well-being.

AFFIRM

20 Positive I AM Laughing Affirmations to help bring more laughter and joy into your life:

1. I AM finding humor in everyday situations and embracing laughter.

2. I AM allowing myself to laugh freely and without inhibition.

3. I AM enjoying life's funny moments and sharing laughter with others.

4. I AM laughing often and bringing joy to those around me.

5. I AM seeking out comedy, funny movies, and jokes to boost my mood.

6. I AM embracing the healing power of laughter in my life.

7. I AM appreciating life's absurdities and laughing at them.

8. I AM letting go of stress and tension through laughter.

9. I AM spreading laughter and happiness wherever I go.

10. I AM surrounding myself with people who make me laugh and feel good.

11. I AM learning to laugh at myself and not take life too seriously.

12. I AM noticing the funny side of life and embracing it.

13. I AM releasing my fears and worries through laughter.

14. I AM using laughter to connect with others and create positive memories.

15. I AM finding joy and amusement in the little things.

16. *I AM cultivating a playful attitude and enjoying life to the fullest.*

17. *I AM embracing laughter as a natural stress-reliever.*

18. *I AM celebrating the power of laughter to uplift and inspire.*

19. *I AM laughing my way to a happier, healthier, and more positive life.*

20. *I AM cherishing the laughter-filled moments and carrying them with me.*

Incorporate these affirmations into your daily routine, and you'll likely find yourself laughing

more often and enjoying the benefits of laughter. Remember that laughter is contagious, so

share it with others to spread happiness and positivity.

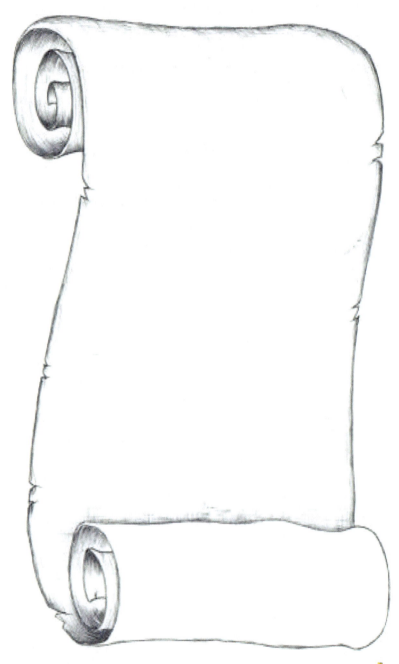

LOLITA'S

LUSCIOUS

LEMONADE

LETTERS

OF

LOVE

January 2, 2008

Bernie Mac

Dear Mr. Mac,

I owe you one from last year. Last year I had just gotten out of the hospital after having an angiogram and a work up for chest pains that the doctors thought were heart related.

Mr. Mac, I'm in recovery right now due to a surgery that I just had and I'm watching you on television being interviewed by Tavis Smiley. I'm sitting here with a smile on my face during your entire interview.

It's a beautiful thing to watch you Mr. Mac, I just love and appreciate you, your talent, your wit, and charisma. It's a beautiful thing for me to be sitting here being entertained by such a beautiful black man as I'm hearing you say that, "if you make someone laugh then you've done your job!"

Last year I didn't take the time out to sit down and write to you and say thank you for making me laugh a year ago Mr. Bernie Mac. Thank you for staying true to your craft, your gifts and talents reign supreme. You're an artist and you bring joy to my life. When you're on I stop what I'm doing to watch, listen, laugh, feel good and in between the good stuff I seek the opportunity to learn. You're a teacher, you lead by example and for that I applaud you Mr. Mac. Today, I am writing to you because I will not let another moment go by without saying Bernie Mac, "thank you!"

I feel good right now in my soul and spirit. Last year when I was having all those tests and procedures they were looking in my chest because my chest was hurting but it was actually my breast that had the pain. A few months after your interview was aired I was diagnosed with breast cancer. Since then Mr. Mac I've had a mastectomy in my left chest. My surgery was September 28, 2007.

Today I have a pre-op appointment with my doctor for reconstruction surgery. A lot of thoughts of doubts, fears and anxiety are trying to creep into my psyche and over take my emotions due to my upcoming surgery scheduled on January 8, 2008. I have a saying that I only give the devil 15 minutes a day and with those fifteen minutes if I need to cry, I'll cry. If I need to shout, kick, throw, bite, what have you, I'll do it within any given fifteen minutes throughout the course of any given day but that's it! No more. I consciously make sure that I don't give place to anything negative any longer than that in a twenty four hour time frame.

When I came home tonight I caught the end of the "Kings of Comedy" and from the moment you came out on stage I have not stopped laughing! I have warm fuzzie wuzzies on the inside of me screaming with joy………I knew that I would not let another second pass me by without picking up my pen and journal to tell you how much joy you've given me over the years.

Mr. Bernie Mac, thank you. Thank you for being here with me at this time in my life when I need joy and laughter. Thank you for being obedient, brave and courageous to step out in faith and follow the call God placed on your life to bring his children joy! It feels so good to hear you talk about relatives and offer up humor to the things that happen in each one of our lives yet you express in ways that only you can do. You are the comedic postman, thank you for the delivery.

I have always been a "Bernie Mac Girl!"

P.S. Since the writing of this excerpt from one of my journals, Mr. Bernie Mac is no longer with us and has gone on to rest in the hands of the almighty. I also would like to express to the Bernie Mac family that I do believe in the power of laughter to aid in healing of the body, mind and soul and please know that your loved one was a carrier of all things good and wonderful. He truly blessed my soul and spirit while I was battling cancer and for that I will forever be grateful. I offer my sincere condolences to his family and friends and would like to say that Mr. Bernie Mac is truly missed and may he rest in peace.

Love Always,

Lolita Jackson

January 31, 2008

Ellen Degeneress

Dear Ellen,

I am writing to you today to say "Thank You!" Ellen, I'm going to try and get this out to you as best I can. I was already having a horrible morning and today has been one of those days that I can't put my finger on. I had just gotten off the telephone talking to a friend of mine telling her that I was going through some things ya know, at that moment I felt as if my world was collapsing around me. I gave her my 15 minute rant and then some!

So Ellen, it all started with a cup of coffee. You see Ellen I wanted another cup of coffee….. My husband Stephen went out this morning and bought me a cup of americano before he left for work but he didn't have enough money to bring home a jumbo cup and then he left out the door and off to work he went and it wasn't until he left that I realized that one cup of coffee would not suffice. I was in need of another cup of coffee to satisfy my three cups of coffee per day habit or my one jumbo cup of coffee per day gotta have my fix, shi*!

Anyway Ellen, so Stephen's gone and around 7:45 a.m. I started feigning for another cup of coffee! I had no car, and mind you I'm still in recovery from surgery which also kept me from walking to the coffee house. So, I asked my neighbor to pick me up a cup of coffee while being out on the drop the kid at school morning ritual who I saw getting into their car to take their child to school. I was told no because other children had to be picked up this particular morning. So, in the meantime I saw that my other neighbor was starting up their car to take their child to school so I asked the same question, "neighbor, will you pick me up a cup of coffee for me from the coffee house while you're out and about

130

taking your child to school?" I was told no again. My neighbor could not accommodate me and my coffeeness!

Ellen, all I know is as I was walking back into the house it all hit me like a ton of bricks! "WHAM!"

You see Ellen about 4 days ago our car got picked up by the repo man. You know, my beautiful china white jaguar with the platinum kitty on the hood was picked up in the middle of the night. Now Ellen somewhere in my imagination, my head, my thoughts of temporary insanity, I believed, I mean I really thought that it wasn't the end of the world and I was going to be able to handle it. How soon did reality catch up with me and what was going on in my head and in my life were headed for a collision of epic proportions! All of a sudden life was starting to suck big time. You see Ellen prior to today I wouldn't have needed to ask anyone to get me anything because I would have been able to get it for myself! But now, right now at this very minute I'm in my feelings, my feelings that want to cry, my feelings that hurt and are in pain, my feelings that wish this was all some sort of bad dream, my feelings that has to feel this bullshit, my feelings that want to curse, but who do I curse? My feelings that feels like my skin is crawling with stinging red ants dipped in cayenne pepper set ablaze inside my veins and every muscle, cell and fiber of my very existence because now I'm realizing that I won't be getting that cup of coffee and also, I DON"T HAVE MY CAR and what's worse, don't nobody give a shit! In fact, for all intents and purposes their stares kind of feel like part of them look and feel like they are happy that I don't have my car (bitch you was doing way too much anyway driving around with that jaguar living in a rented townhouse!) But, that's for another book, right!!! Soooo Ellen, I'm also drowning in my sorrowful tears of embarrassment, shame, guilt and pity. Right now, I'm pitifully hurting. I want to be mad too Ellen…..I want to be mad at my sister because when I asked her to borrow some money to pay my last car note she said that people buy what they want and beg for what they need. She said that it doesn't make much sense to be driving a jag and be renting a townhouse so part of me agreed that I wasn't worthy of the jag and decided subconsciously that she was right and I didn't deserve the car because I don't even own a home and Ellen who would do that? Who would go out and buy a luxury car and not even have a mortgage? All of this is trapping me in my thoughts, all of this has me cornered, all of this has an all too familiar tune that says, "Lolita, baby girl, your life is fucked!" God, you better come quickly and you bettah come now! God, don't you hear me? God, don't you see me? God, why? Really God? Damn, Ellen, if I just would have had that cup of coffee none of these feelings would have surfaced. The cup of coffee would have fixed ALL of this! I mean wouldn't it Ellen? I mean right Ellen? Hellooooo, Ellen? Ellen, are you there? I mean that is what you're there for right? You are the judge, jury and fixer of all things wrong with this world right? I mean Ellen I need you to take over where Oprah left off and say, "Lolita, you get a car, you get a car, Lolita, my beloved lovely baby girl, here are your keys and you my baby girl, wake up because you get a got blessed, muther fuckn, got damn, muther fuckn car!" Ellennnnnnnnnnnnnnn! Stop this ride………Let me off this fuckn rollercoaster of emotional bullshit! My heart hurts and it is crying tears that are dripping in black blood!

I'm in pain and I want a cup of COFFEE!!!!! I can feel myself having a complete meltdown. I can feel the walls closing in on me. It feels as if my whole battle with breast cancer is about to culminate and crescendo, climaxing in epic proportions with me jumping off the nearest bridge if I don't get andwith me not being able to get a cup of motherfucking coffee! Physically I feel like crap in pain from surgery and emotionally on a runaway train heading for and through the tunnel of doom, gloom & misery….. I am feeling needy and I am hating this feeling with every fiber of my being. Shit, doggone it, this is not going to be good. Inside my body, my brain, my mind and I keep saying to me "Lolita, if you can just get a cup of coffee everything will be okay!" "Lolitahhhh, Lolitahhhh, dooodooodoooodooodooo, freddy cruger music playing in the background of emotional and psychological terror! Then I did the ultimate, you know the ultimate charge, the charge to myself that says play the blame game Lolita. You know the "it's them, it's those people, the people who said they would be here for me and it's those people who I haven't asked them for anything and because I haven't asked them for anything when I do they should oblige, right Ellen because don't get me wrong, I'm clearly not confused they did offer and the ONE TIME I ASK they aren't here for me people and they should be even if I ask last minute regardless of what's going on in their lives people, right now it's about Lolita, her world, her feelings and o yeah, don't forget her cancer diagnosis, surgery, pain, blah, blah, blah, blah, blah!. Ellen, are you there, did I lose you? You are still listening to me right Ellen? So Ellen, now I'm feeling sorry for myself and I am spiraling & spinning out. I'm on this rollercoaster and there is no getting off until and when I get that cup of coffee!

So Ellen, I called my daughter who was in another state crying telling her about how horrible I feel and how NOBODY is here for me because they all have lives and they weren't going to be able to stop what they were doing and in the middle of their morning to go and get me a cup of coffee. Also keep in mind that one of the neighbors I asked was a devoutly religious whose religion didn't even allow the consumption of caffeinated beverages, yet I was all in my feelings disregarding any of that. I NEED, and have to have a cup of coffee! Needless to say I lost it when my daughter suggested that I have a cup of tea! Say what? Really Mary, okay! "Crescendo!" "Whoop, there it is!" #aintnobodygottimeforthat girl!

I sat here crying, crying and crying some more, now I decide to pray for my health, pray for strength and definitely pray that I'll never let this happen to me again Lord, you know that prayer that says and we all have prayed it, "If you bless me this one time, if you get me out of this one thing, Lord, Father, I PROMISE, I'll never, Right?

I started thinking, if only I could walk, or ride my bike???? I would get it myself! If only I didn't have all of these medical bills then I would still have my car, blah, blah, blah, blah, blah!

So Ellen, what did I do? Yep, you guessed it, I called a cab to take me 10 blocks to get a cup of coffee. We sat in the drive through and waited for the line to go down and when we got to the window I ordered a cup of coffee from the back seat of a cab!!! The barista knew who I was and yet she never said a word, she just looked at me as if I had two heads sitting in the back of that cab ordering one cup of coffee. Now Ellen, if that wasn't bad enough, it wasn't until I got home that I realized that I purchased the smallest cup of coffee they had! I didn't even order a jumbo coffee and by the time this fiasco, escapade was over I just bought the most expensive cup of coffee known to man!

As I sat in my window, torturing myself watching my neighbors come and go freely I started thinking they could care less about me and then your show came on and today you featured the "Tribe of Judah Choir!" What did I do? I hit the floor! I fell to my knees and cried, cried, cried like a little baby. I can't stop crying now trying to write this to you. My tears are tears of JOY! Again, as bad as I was feeling and as bad as things FEEL......I know that God is showing me how much he loves me by putting this choir on your show and then when you started dancing to Kirk Franklin "What?" That did for me Ellen, I was cooked after that! When "Stomp" came on and Kirk said "Lately I've been going through some things that's really got me down, I need someone, somebody to help me turn my life around. I can't explain it. I can't obtain it. Jesus your love is so

134

amazing. You can't take my joy, devil. It makes me want to stomp, dance and clap my hands!" Ellen, Thank You! No weapon formed against me shall prosper. Not only did I let it all out but I know that God used you and your show to wipe my tears away. I am indebted to you forever Miss Ellen Degeneress! Thank You Ellen for extending his hands! Ellen, thank you for saving me with your obedience! I Love You Ellen, I will always keep you in my prayers. Miss Ellen you will always have a warrior standing in the gap for you and with you in the spirit, praying that you'll continually be blessed!

Much Love,

    I Love You

        Your sister in the spirit,

           Lolita

February 6, 2008

Louise Hay

Dear Louise Hay,

Thank you for your book, "You Can Heal Yourself!" One day, not long ago, a few months ago to be exact. I was in Barnes & Noble having a complete meltdown about being diagnosed with cancer and to add to my woes I had just lost my journal and I had just lost my husband in the store which was not good, I mean it was not good at all as I stood in the middle of the store losing it, and that's putting it mildly, okay I f'n lost it as I began to call out my husband's name in this quiet book store with a library's atmosphere as onlookers looked in astonishment and amazement as I continued to ball out with tears from "Niagara Falls" and one of the most bewildered looks of panic and frustration imaginable on my face only to be approached by one of the nicest, kindest ladies on the planet with the softest voice I've ever heard tell me without one question?????

"You need to read these…!"

I looked down and one of the books was your book, "You Can Heal Yourself!" I immediately knew that God had a plan for my life and I instinctively knew that I was going to win, and be healed. Me being in that store at that moment was all part of God's divine intervention and the law of attraction and I knew that I was operating in the secret behind the secret.

The universal laws were in operation with the vibration and energy frequency that I was in tuned to and it was a magnetic force field that was charged with love and healing and I received it with open arms!

I must say "Thank You!"

Love you much,
Thanks for your obedience and for answering the call to serve,

In Solidarity, Lolita

February 7, 2008

Robin Roberts

Dearest Robin,

I can't stop crying right now. I watched I dare you, and when you walked out onto the stage with that beautiful gown and your shaved head embracing your moment, time and experience with cancer, I just kept crying.

You are so beautiful and you're absolutely right, we all are going through something. Right now I'm going through reconstruction after a mastectomy on September 28, 2007.

This is who I am today. I too believe we can climb our mountains in life.

Thank you for your courage and for being so brave for all of us to see. I've been watching you for months and admiring you from afar as you push through the tears and joy of the whole cancer experience. I watch you on television as the epitome of beauty both inside and out.

Thank you for allowing us to share this journey with you. I remember when you said you woke up and Diane Sawyer was there holding your hand after surgery. I remember when I woke up after my mastectomy surgery to see my husband, daughter, and grandson. I'll never forget the joy I felt to know that they were there waiting for me in recovery!

Again, thank you Robin, may God continue *to Bless You,*
Love Always,

Lolita

Monday, February 25, 2008

Stephen Jackson

My Dearest Darling Stephen,

Today baby my thanks goes out to you again! Stephen, I am calling you my, "Superman Jackson!" Baby, you are amazing. Here we are again faced with another surgery, #5 in 5 months. We just got to the place where you can work again and get a full paycheck without needing help from other people and then this happens.

What do you do? You roll up your sleeves and you stand in the gap and you're right here supporting me. No complaints, just standing in the gap for and with me. Today you took the time, in the middle of everything going on, to make phone calls for Sir Stephen and have him go to a tutor, then you came back to the hospital. I am so amazed and in awe of you that I am documenting what your day has been like because I don't want to ever forget what you do for me, have done for me and what you do for us and have done for us as a family! I want to always be able to look back to this day, this moment and remind myself of your amazing qualities just in case one day I get on some tangent and forget just how amazing and wonderful my husband REALLY is! I have to write down everything that I've witnessed today with my own two eyes because if I don't I would leave out a detail here or a detail there. So, here it goes, this is the day you had today!

You spent the night at the hospital and you left at 6 a.m., then took Sir Stephen home so he could go to school to be at school by 7:30 a.m. You packed me a hospital bag with my toiletries and came back to the hospital by 10 a.m. On the way back to the hospital you stopped at Barnes & Noble to buy me a book. You visited me at the hospital, helped me with my showering, grooming, hair and making sure my room looked presentable just in case someone came to visit

139

because you know I would freak out about a messy room instead of just lying here relaxing. You left me at 3 p.m. to go and pick up Sir Stephen. You made some business calls from the house and then you left the house to go to the bank. You remembered that you forgot to hit the record button at the house for something that you wanted to see later and you got off the freeway, went back to the house and then got back on the freeway and came back to the hospital so that I could see Sir Stephen. You and Sir Stephen visited me and then you left to take Sir Stephen to his tutor, after that you and Sir Stephen came back to the hospital he slept and you left here to go take care of another personal matter only to return by 6 a.m. to start all over again. It's 8:30 a.m. the next day as I have just documented a miracle! Steve Jackson,

I Love You, I will NEVER forget what you mean to me, and I don't know if you know just how much I love and appreciate you. These moments are forever etched into my spirit, mind, body and soul. That is why I just wrote all of this down so that if I ever get on some brand newness, I will remind myself of your selflessness and how you ride for me and with me.

Much love to you Mr. Jackson
Forever,
Mrs. Lolita Jackson

By Mary Dyton (Daughter)

Today has been an emotional roller coaster. I'm trying to be strong for my mom, being positive and optimistic but at the same time it's affecting me a lot. I don't really know what to think besides that, what is happening sucks. I'm sad for her, this whole thing has happened so fast and unexpected, it feels so surreal. I know that everything is going to be okay, but just the thought of my mother having breast cancer and having to remove her breast doesn't sit right with me or my heart. If something was to happen to her I don't know how I could go on? I understand how my brother feels the way he does and doesn't wanna be around it, but I kinda feel that way too but I know I have to be there with her and for her every second. My son being here helps me not be so down but when they wheel her off I know I am going to lose it!

Until she returns (Smiley Face)

Sincerely,
Mary Dyton

By Stephen Jackson

As I'm waiting for Lo to see her doctor before surgery deep down inside I can't wait for this to be over with. I feel tired. I really don't want this to happen but I know it will save her life and more than anything I need her alive. It starts (her surgery) at 3:00 and it feels like it is taking forever, as I am looking into her eyes I know she knows that I Love Her and can't wait for this to be over because I know after this she will be taking off!

Love you Lo,

-Stephen

My Dearest Sir Stephen,

Vonrizzle, Rizzle Drizzle (Just so you don't forget who you are!)

I am writing you this letter with a whole lot of thoughts in my mind and not being sure of how to say everything that I'm thinking. Of course, first and foremost I want you to be reading this letter many, many, many, many years from now with yourself and your family. Speaking of family, I see you in your future as a proud father and husband of many, many, many, children, just as proud of your children as I am of you.

Sir Stephen, I know that my diagnosis hasn't been easy for you having to process the initial shock and fear of hearing that I have breast cancer, it's a bit surreal for me so I know how you must feel. I have insisted that you keep your schedule as if nothing has happened. I know it's hard for you to keep playing sports, stay focused in school, deal with friends and family, trying to eat dinner, so forth and so on, but son hear me when I tell you this, your foundation has prepared you to handle whatever life sends your way.

Do you hear me? I know it's emotional, you're strong, you're independent, you're a thinker and problem solver, you will hold up under this immense pressure, I know that, my faith and your faith has been the bricks that are paving your way to walk on, build upon, Sir Stephen, you got this.

Now son, I want you to CRY! I don't think that you know it's okay to CRY! I cry all of the time, you need to cry. Crying allows you to cleanse your emotions and feelings. Crying helps you release your fears, worries and anxieties, crying also makes room for your cup to fill back up. I know it's not popular to cry as a young man but you need to okay? One day you'll be an adult, don't be that adult man who thinks it's not cool or okay to cry. Let it out, sit with your feelings, you can't drink them away, drug them away, smoke them

143

away or eat them away. Sir Stephen crying is your gateway to clarity, with your tears you'll find solace, comfort and strength. When it gets tough and believe me before it's all over it'll get tougher, just know you don't need to wear a mask. Please Vonrae, find someone you trust to share your feelings with, allow yourself to explore all options for positive ways to handle all of what I am going through, will go through, and most importantly what you're going through...

I need you to keep your life on track as if, keep playing sports, keep listening to music, stay with good friends, keep dancing, keep playing with your dog, stay active. Your body is built like your dad's. One day you'll be a gym rat! I want you to move on to highschool do you hear me? I want you to graduate, go to college, get married, and you know what? I will be here to see it and experience it with you...

I love you, Sir Stephen

P.S. Keep laughing and watching Martin Lawrence!

Loving you more than forever, And, forever more I'll always love you...

My Dearest Mary Tieriese Alischa Dyton, (smile)

I Love You! Mary, thank you for being here with me, thank you for being here for me. Thank you, thank you, thank you, thank you for Nazzawaz! Mary, you have made me the happiest grandma in the world! Nazier is so deliciously handsome and he's here, all mine to enjoy bringing me comfort and strength. When I look at you Mary, I see one of the strongest women that I know. You are here, helping Stephen and Sir Stephen in ways that I'm sure they didn't even realize that they needed help in... I need you here Mary, I'm so grateful and so thankful because you are now a mother with a job and family of your own so don't think that I take this lightly.

I am lying here in this hospital bed looking at you, looking into your eyes over here writing into this journal about you, you have no idea what I'm writing but I can see your concern for me. I can see your worry for me. Mary, don't worry about me, I want you to live your best life. One of the happiest days of my life was the day I woke up in the hospital room and your dad had on a hospital gown with a pink button on it that said, "I had a girl and her name is Mary!" I was just coming out of anesthesia and I remember looking up at him and I said, "A girl, for real, Mary, you named her Mary?" He replied, "Yes!" That was the biggest smile ever on his face. The second happiest moment was at your graduation from college, I was so happy I didn't know what to do Teresa... So Mary, no matter what happens, just know that you are a good woman, you are a great mother and daughter. I want you to go as far as you want to go in this world. Go get your Master's Degree, buy that Mercedes SUV that you want, travel the world Teresa and take Nazzawaz to DisneyLand.

Nazier is so cute, cuter than Andre' even though Andre is super fine, sorry Nazzawaz is just a little bit cuter.

Thank you for standing in the gap for me, nursing my wounds, cooking and cleaning. It's more than I can ask for. Mary, make sure you get your mammograms, start getting them in your thirties, don't wait like I did. If you see a black discharge or any kind of discharge coming from your breast nipples, run to the doctor to get it checked out. I almost waited too late to get the discharge in my breasts checked. I overlooked it as just residue from breastfeeding. I guess that's what I told myself, now realizing there's no such foolish thing! Also, Teresa, start touching your breasts, get to know them, touch your body Mary, love your body Mary. I want you to love your body better than anyone else can or will. Don't be afraid of what you see in the mirror, embrace your body, embrace yourself Mary okay...

I Love you, be happy Teresa, keep smiling Teresa

P.S. Thank you for being my advocate, you're the best there is... Loving you more than forever, And forever more, I'll always love you! Mom.

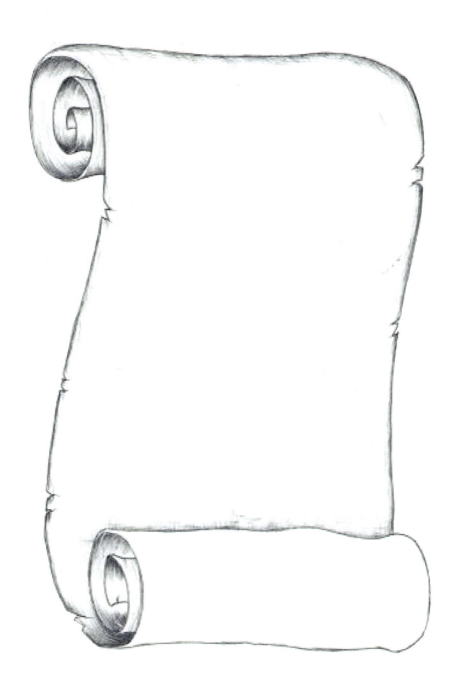

20. WALK

("Hey, hey, hey, it's ya girl, Lo Lo from PO!
#WalkingWomenWin! #Lolita'sLusciousLemonade!") That statement is
how I would ALWAYS introduce myself as I uploaded a walking video
vlog onto my social media FB account! I started walking and kept
walking, mostly to free my mind and for the cool fresh Pacific Northwest
Air! I started a daily blog to talk about my walks out in nature and
describe what getting out of the house meant for my mental health at the
time, nothing more, nothing less. I needed an outlet and I meant that
literally, I was in an apartment and I needed out! I would write ALL of
the time by free hand, which somehow turned into a blog and it's in the
blog that I just kept writing and walking and wanting to tell other women,
hello, let's go! When I initially started walking and claiming
#walkingwomenwin It never occurred to me until years later about the
true actual/factual health benefits of walking and how instrumental
walking is for our health!

Walking therapy can provide numerous physical benefits for
breast cancer patients, including improved cardiovascular health,
increased strength and endurance, and better overall physical function.

Walking therapy can be incorporated into a patient's breast cancer recovery plan in a variety of ways, depending on the patient's individual needs and preferences. I incorporated walking into my recovery plan unintentionally, as a patient I included my videos which you can call a way to track my progress but I actually was just showing how I was feeling better, the goal was daily and wanting to stay motivated. I will say this that for me,

embracing walking therapy as a part of my recovery plan with breast cancer it allowed me to take

an active role in my own healing in order to achieve better overall outcomes.

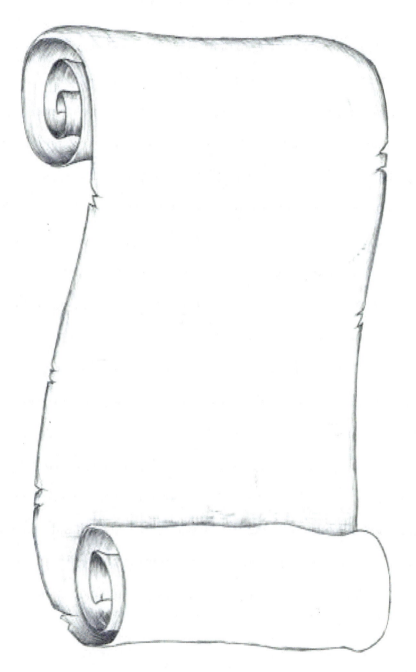

21. BREATHE

After mastectomy, I experienced a range of physical symptoms, such as pain, stiffness, and limited range of motion in the chest and shoulder area. Deep breathing exercise therapy is a non-pharmacological intervention that can help women manage these symptoms and improve their quality of life after mastectomy. In this I want to talk about the benefits of deep breathing. We will discuss the benefits of deep breathing exercise therapy for mastectomy, the mechanism of action, and its safety and effectiveness. But first, let me say here that as I am writing this section I'm noticing a pattern of synchronicities that has happened in my life. I'm having a moment right now, excuse me for a second…

I'm back, let me explain, when I was a young girl in my early twenties I bought a book and VHS video tape by Raquel Welch about Hatha Yoga, now at the time I don't think I ever seen anyone do yoga, if fact, if I'm being honest somewhere in my religion yoga was frowned upon as some sort of hoodoo/woodoo. I bought the book mostly because again I love books, and Raquel Welch was on the cover, it didn't matter what her glossy beautiful book had inside, it presented well… Little did I know that I was being set up for the beginning of my understanding of the benefits of deep breathing. I was too young to grasp the full realm of what the Universe had planned for me down the road, but I was in the building. Let's say my steps had been ordered… Later, meaning many years later, I got further into the benefits of deep breathing by doing breathing exercises daily, I started to help me flatten my stomach, but something started happening to my brain and body as I filled my lungs and body with air/oxygen, it was a natural high that I now can't find one word to explain it. I got one, euphoric… After my diagnosis with breast cancer it came full circle, why I would so easily and readily incorporate deep breathing as a healing modality in recovery and holistic longevity.

Deep breathing exercise therapy involves slow, rhythmic breathing techniques that help regulate the body's autonomic nervous system. The autonomic nervous system is responsible for regulating various bodily functions, such as heart rate, blood pressure, and breathing. After mastectomy, women may experience anxiety, fear, and depression, which can affect the autonomic nervous system's functioning. Deep breathing exercises can help activate the parasympathetic nervous system, which is responsible for the body's rest and relaxation response. This, in turn, can reduce stress, anxiety, and pain, and improve overall well-being.

There are several types of deep breathing exercise therapy that can be used after mastectomy. One of the most common techniques is diaphragmatic breathing, which involves breathing from the abdomen rather than the chest. This technique can help reduce tension in the chest and shoulder area and improve overall breathing capacity. Another technique is pursed-lip breathing,which involves exhaling slowly through pursed lips, as if blowing out a candle. This technique can help reduce shortness of breath and improve lung function. Other techniques include alternate nostril breathing, progressive muscle relaxation, and guided imagery.

Deep breathing exercise therapy can be easily implemented in the post-mastectomy rehabilitation program. Patients can be taught the techniques during the hospital stay and encouraged to continue practicing them at home. A physical therapist or respiratory therapist can guide patients in choosing the appropriate technique and provide feedback on proper form and technique. Patients can also use audio and video resources to practice the techniques on their own. Deep breathing exercise therapy is a safe and effective intervention that can be used as part of a comprehensive rehabilitation program after mastectomy. Consult your physician.

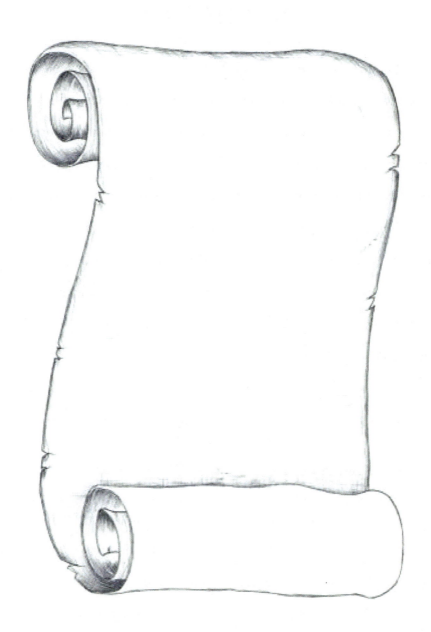

22. SOUNDS

Sound therapy involves the use of sound to heal and restore balance in the body. Therapeutic healing frequencies are specific frequencies that have been shown to have healing properties. In recent years, the use of sound therapy and healing frequencies has gained popularity in the field of cancer treatment, particularly for breast cancer.

Sound therapy has been shown to have several potential benefits for breast cancer patients. It can help to reduce stress, anxiety, and depression, which are common psychological effects of cancer diagnosis and treatment. Additionally, sound therapy can help to reduce pain, improve sleep quality, and enhance overall well-being.

Therapeutic healing frequencies are specific frequencies that have been shown to have healing properties. They can be used to help reduce inflammation, promote cell regeneration, and stimulate the immune system.

The use of sound therapy and healing frequencies is not a new concept, but it is only recently that the scientific community has started to investigate its potential benefits. Studies have shown that sound therapy can have a positive impact on the body at a cellular level, including reducing inflammation and promoting cell regeneration.

Sound therapy can be delivered in a variety of ways, including through music, singing bowls, tuning forks, and binaural beats. Each of these techniques has its own unique benefits and applications. For breast cancer patients, sound therapy can be incorporated into their treatment plans as complementary therapy alongside traditional cancer treatments.

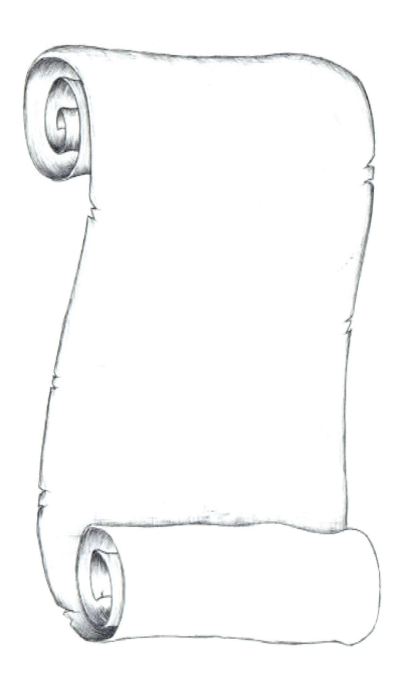

23. MALIBU

I can tell you first hand that the ocean saved me! The Pacific Ocean is my boo! Pacific Coast Highway is my boyfriend! I AM IN LOVE! I went to California, woke up in Malibu and knew in my soul that I was home. I had never been, nothing inside me desired to go, but if being asked as a four year old what do you want to be when you grow up by your dad and you say, "Oceanographer" not ever hearing the word before, I rest my case! (True Story) My dad used to tell me that story, but somehow I remembered it! I remember being at the beach as a little girl, hearing the sea gulls, feeling the ice cold water on my bare tiny feet, seeing that big rock in the water, thinking, and having a sense of belonging. Malibu, met me there, another full circle moment I was having on earth. Now, grant it again, I had NO CLUE about all the scientific, mental, and physical benefits of this journey that I started to discover, peel back the layers of what I was truly experiencing, and wait. I didn't put this in the lemon chapter but let's not forget I showed up in California and lemons were on trees EVERYWHERE! I promise I cried tears of disbelief and joy! It wasn't until I saw the travesty of the lemons on the grounds from people's trees that I thought, "Say it ain't so!" I was paying almost $100 for a box of little lemons, where God sent me the lemons that are the size of grapefruits for free! Back to the ocean… I slowly started to learn after a few years in California, kicking it in Malibu, (catch that name drop) that the ocean water contains many minerals and nutrients that can have therapeutic effects on the body. The high salt content of the ocean water can help to detoxify the body and boost the immune system, which can be especially beneficial for breast cancer patients who may have

weakened immune systems due to chemotherapy or radiation therapy.the magnesium in the ocean water can help to reduce stress and promote relaxation, which can be helpful for managing anxiety and depression associated with breast cancer.

Negative ions are abundant near the ocean, and they have been shown to have a variety of health benefits. They can also improve the body's ability to absorb oxygen, which can be helpful for patients undergoing chemotherapy or radiation therapy. Additionally, negative ions have been shown to have anti-inflammatory properties, which can be helpful for reducing inflammation and swelling after mastectomy.

For women who are scheduled to undergo mastectomy, spending time near the ocean can be a helpful way to prepare for the procedure.

Ocean water therapy and negative ion therapy can be especially beneficial for patients who may be feeling overwhelmed or fearful about the upcoming surgery.

Additionally, spending time near the ocean can help patients to feel more connected to nature, which can be helpful for promoting a sense of calm and peace.

After undergoing mastectomy, many women experience a range of physical and emotional symptoms, including pain, fatigue, and anxiety.

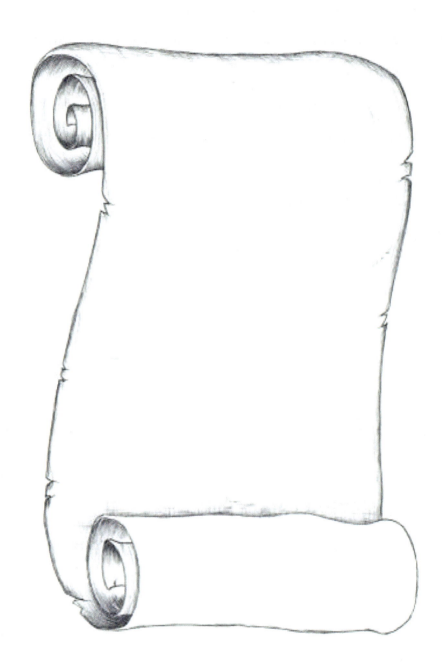

24. SPIRIT

Spiritual health refers to a person's overall well-being in their spiritual dimension. It involves having a sense of meaning, purpose, and connection to something greater than oneself.

Spiritual health is important because it affects a person's emotional and physical health, relationships, and overall quality of life.

Spirituality can provide comfort and support during times of fear and anxiety. It can help women find a sense of peace and acceptance, even in the face of uncertainty. Prayer, meditation, and mindfulness can be helpful in managing anxiety and stress.

Breast cancer can cause a woman to question her purpose and meaning in life. Spiritual health can help women find meaning and purpose in their experience. It can help them see their cancer journey as an opportunity for growth and transformation.

Spirituality can provide a sense of community and connection to others. Support groups, spiritual retreats, and other activities can help women connect with others who share their experience.

Spiritual health can help women build resilience and cope with the challenges of breast cancer treatment. Practices like gratitude, forgiveness, and self-compassion can help women find strength and resilience during difficult times.

Practices like journaling, scripting and visualization can be helpful in clarifying goals and intentions.

Spiritual health can help women transition back to life after breast cancer treatment. It can help them find meaning and purpose in their survivorship journey. Volunteer work and community service can be helpful in building a sense of purpose and connection.

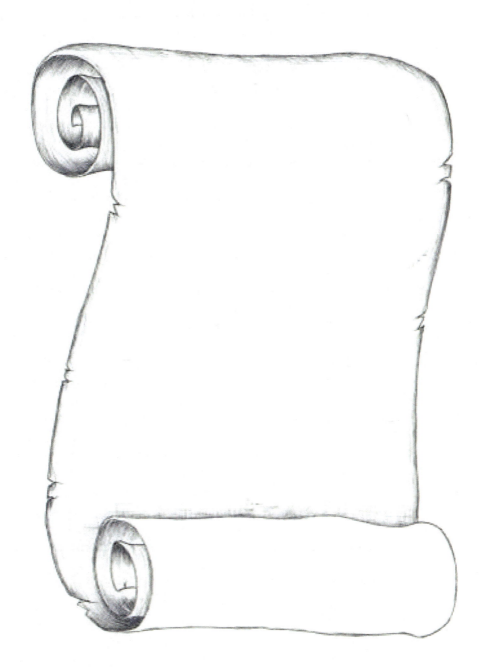

25. OXYGEN

Hyperbaric Oxygen Therapy (HBOT) is a non-invasive medical treatment that involves breathing pure oxygen in a pressurized chamber. It is used to treat a variety of medical conditions, including wounds that are slow to heal. After mastectomy, HBOT can be used to promote healing and reduce the risk of complications, such as infection and tissue damage.

During HBOT, patients lie in a pressurized chamber and breathe 100% oxygen, which increases the amount of oxygen in their blood and tissues. This increased oxygen can help stimulate the growth of new blood vessels, reduce inflammation, and promote the production of collagen, which is essential for tissue repair. HBOT is generally safe and well-tolerated, but it may have some side effects, such as ear discomfort and temporary changes in vision.

HBOT can be used after mastectomy to help promote healing and reduce the risk of complications. In particular, HBOT can help prevent infection, reduce swelling, and promote the growth of healthy tissue. One of the major benefits of HBOT after mastectomy is its ability to reduce the risk of infection. After mastectomy, the risk of infection is increased due to the surgical incision and the presence of drains. HBOT can help reduce this risk by promoting the growth of healthy tissue and increasing blood flow to the affected area, which helps deliver immune cells and nutrients to the site of the surgery. HBOT can also help reduce swelling and inflammation after mastectomy. Swelling and inflammation can be painful and can slow down the healing process. HBOT can help reduce swelling by promoting lymphatic drainage and reducing inflammation by increasing the amount of oxygen in the tissues.

Finally, HBOT can help promote the growth of healthy tissue after mastectomy. This is important because the surgical incision can damage the surrounding tissue, and it is important to promote the growth of new tissue to fill in the gap left by the surgery. HBOT can stimulate the production of collagen, which is essential for tissue repair, and can also help promote the growth of new blood vessels, which are important for delivering nutrients and oxygen to the affected area.

HBOT is a promising treatment option for patients who have undergone mastectomy. I to this day participate in HBOT!

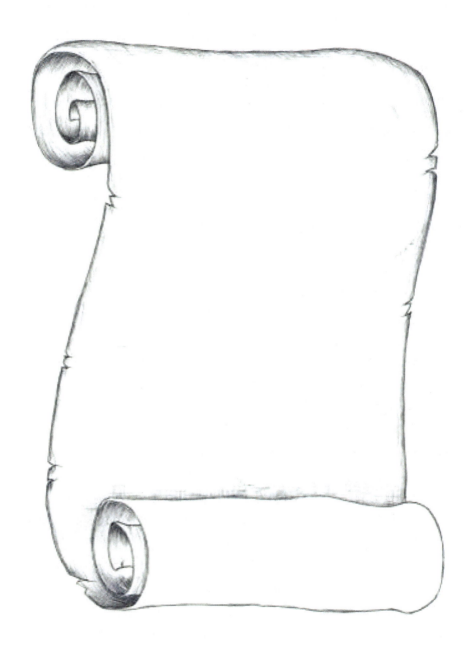

26. SUN

I grew up in the Pacific Northwest, hence Lo Lo from PO, I used to say I had cancer three times in Seattle. Now, I say, I was healed three times in Seattle. Seattle clearly did right by me, but the natural Vitamin D from the sun was calling my name. Hello Malibu, here I come, there I went! Again, another one of those moments that I truly didn't have a lot of facts or details, my spirit said go, and I went. I am learning and have learned that sunshine and natural Vitamin D play an essential role in maintaining good health. Vitamin D is a fat-soluble vitamin that is produced in the skin when it is exposed to ultraviolet B (UVB) radiation from sunlight. It can also be obtained from certain foods and supplements.

Vitamin D is essential for strong bones and teeth as it helps the body absorb calcium and

phosphorus from the diet. It also plays a crucial role in the immune system, as well as in the

regulation of cell growth and differentiation.

One of the most significant benefits of Vitamin D is its role in cancer prevention and treatment.Studies have shown that low levels of

Vitamin D are associated with an increased risk of developing several types of cancer, including breast, colon, and prostate cancer.

In breast cancer, Vitamin D has been found to play a critical role in reducing the risk of developing the disease, as well as improving survival rates among those who have been diagnosed. Research suggests that Vitamin D may help prevent breast cancer by inhibiting the growth of cancer cells and promoting apoptosis, or programmed cell death, in cancer cells.

In addition to its role in cancer prevention, Vitamin D has also been found to be beneficial in the treatment of cancer. Studies have shown that Vitamin D can enhance the effectiveness of chemotherapy and radiation therapy, as well as reduce the side effects of these treatments.

Breast cancer is one of the most common types of cancer among women. It is a disease in which cancer cells form in the tissues of the breast. Risk factors for breast cancer include age, family history, exposure to estrogen, and a lack of physical activity. Symptoms of breast cancer include a lump or thickening in the breast, nipple discharge, and changes in the size or shape of the breast.

In conclusion, sunshine and natural Vitamin D are crucial for maintaining good health, particularly in cancer prevention and treatment. Low levels of Vitamin D have been associated with an increased risk of several types of cancer, including breast cancer. It is important to get enough Vitamin D through a combination of sunshine, diet, and supplements, and to take steps to reduce the risk of developing breast cancer, such as maintaining a healthy weight, exercising regularly, and limiting alcohol consumption.

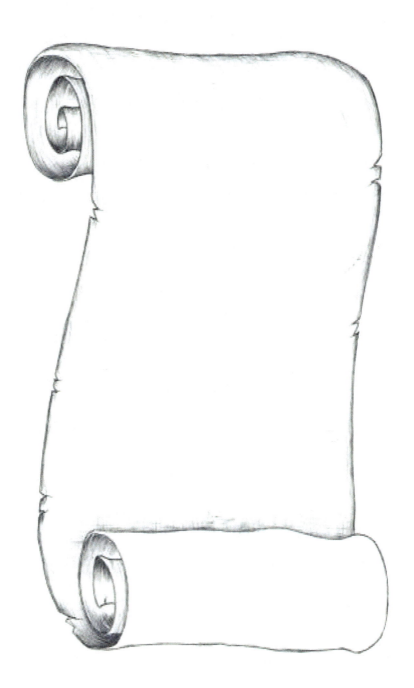

27. LONELINESS

This is a tricky topic, mainly because being alone doesn't always equate to being lonely. For me, I have and still do experience both. Honestly, sometimes I can't move with loneliness, other times I can't wait to be left the heck alone and cherish the opportunity to be so. I believe the reason why I included this chapter is because I know the importance of finding balance, that's the key. I know that a breast cancer diagnosis can be an emotionally isolating experience, which can lead to loneliness. The first step in coping with loneliness is to acknowledge its existence. Many people may not want to admit their loneliness, as they may feel that it is a sign of weakness. However, acknowledging your feelings of loneliness is essential to coping with them. Once you acknowledge your loneliness, you can start to take steps to address it.

One of the most effective ways to cope with loneliness during a breast cancer diagnosis is to reach out for support. This support can come from family members, friends, or a support group. Talking to someone who has been through a similar experience can help you feel less alone. Additionally, joining a support group can help you connect with others who understand what you are going through.

Engaging in hobbies and activities that you enjoy can also help you cope with loneliness during a breast cancer diagnosis. This could include taking up a new hobby, such as painting or gardening, or simply spending time with friends and family doing activities that you love. Engaging in activities that bring you joy can help distract you from your loneliness and provide you with a sense of purpose. I have tried all of the above, and I still do. I did not know that I was a crafter! (Laugh Out Loud!)

Self-care is essential when coping with loneliness during a breast cancer diagnosis. Taking care of your physical, emotional, and mental well-being can help you feel more positive and less alone. This could include getting enough sleep, eating a healthy diet, and exercising regularly. Additionally, taking time for activities that make you feel good, such as taking a warm bath or reading a book, can also help you feel more relaxed and connected.

Finally, if you are struggling to cope with loneliness during a breast cancer diagnosis, it may be helpful to seek professional help. A therapist or counselor can help you process your feelings and provide you with tools to manage your loneliness. Remember, seeking professional help is a sign of strength, not weakness.

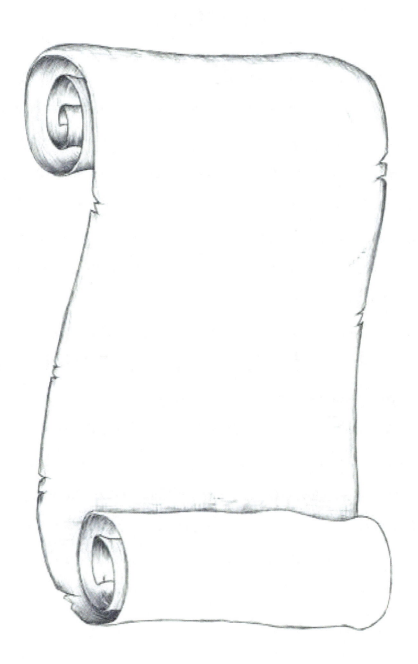

28. ORAL

Oral health is an important aspect of overall health and well-being especially during treatment. Medications, chemo and radiation therapy can send your oral hygiene right down the toilet if you're not careful, trust me. The worst thing that can happen is everyone around you will smell the effects of your treatment right from your tongue and mouth before you, if you're lucky, you'll have someone close to you that loves you enough to tell you that you should probably go to the dentist more the usual twice a year appointments, not have someone buy you packs of gum and breath mints and you say, "O my gosh, thank you, how sweet and thoughtful" all the while it's a hint that you have bad breath oozing out of your pores due to treatment! #truestory!

There are several common oral health issues that people may experience, including cavities, gum disease, and oral cancer. Cavities are caused by bacteria that produce acid, which breaks down the tooth's enamel. Gum disease occurs when plaque builds up on the teeth, leading to inflammation and infection of the gums. Oral cancer can affect any part of the mouth, including the lips, tongue, and throat.

Maintaining good oral health is especially important during breast cancer treatment.

Chemotherapy and radiation therapy can cause side effects such as mouth sores, dry mouth, and infections. These side effects can be managed with proper oral hygiene practices and regular dental checkups.

Body odor can be linked to oral health because bad breath can be caused by bacteria in the mouth. Additionally, gum disease and other oral health issues can lead to inflammation and infection, which can contribute to body odor. To manage body odor, it is important to practice good hygiene, such as showering regularly and using antiperspirant or deodorant, or a lime slice directly onto your arm pit. . Additionally, it may be helpful to wear breathable fabrics and avoid foods that can contribute to body odor.

Oral health is important during breast cancer surgery, as there is a risk of infection. Patients should schedule a dental checkup before surgery and inform their dental provider of their upcoming surgery. Additionally, patients should maintain good oral hygiene practices before and after surgery.

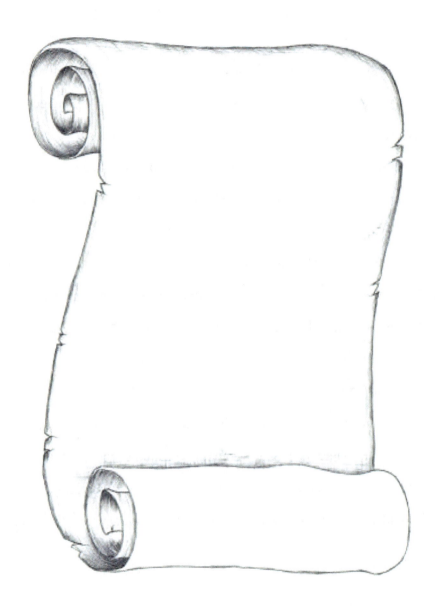

29. LYMPHEDEMA

This is my current experience. Today, I didn't have Lymphedema 16 years ago. The more active I became, the more I had to navigate and manage. I am still learning, moving and scripting my way to the best physical shape and desire I see for my body, that being said, it's also part of experience of calling those things that be not as if it was and navigating my life accordingly, no matter what I'm told, what anyone says or sees in their eyes. Lymphedema is a condition that occurs when lymphatic fluid accumulates in the tissues, causing swelling and discomfort. It is a common complication of breast cancer treatment, particularly after a mastectomy. Post-mastectomy care is an important part of managing lymphedema and involves a range of strategies to help prevent and manage symptoms.

Lymphedema can be caused by damage to the lymphatic system, which may occur as a result of surgery, radiation therapy, or chemotherapy. Symptoms may include swelling in the arms or legs, a feeling of heaviness or tightness, skin changes, and aching or discomfort.

Diagnosing lymphedema typically involves a physical examination and assessment of symptoms.

Other tests, such as lymphoscintigraphy or MRI, may also be used to confirm the diagnosis and determine the severity of the condition.

Prevention strategies for lymphedema include exercise, maintaining a healthy weight, avoiding tight clothing and jewelry, and avoiding activities that may put excess strain on the affected limb. It is also important to take precautions to prevent infection, such as avoiding cuts and burns and practicing good hygiene.

Treatment for lymphedema may include manual lymphatic drainage, compression therapy, exercise, and skin care. In some cases, surgery may be necessary to remove excess tissue or repair damage to the lymphatic system.

Post-mastectomy care involves a range of strategies to promote healing and prevent complications, such as infection and lymphedema. This may include physical therapy, exercises to improve range of motion, and use of compression garments.

Living with lymphedema and undergoing post-mastectomy care can be emotionally challenging. Patients may experience anxiety, depression, or a sense of loss of control over their body. It is important to address these emotional and psychological issues and provide patients with support and resources to cope.

While lymphedema and post-mastectomy care can be challenging, many patients are able to manage their symptoms and lead full and active lives. I AM!

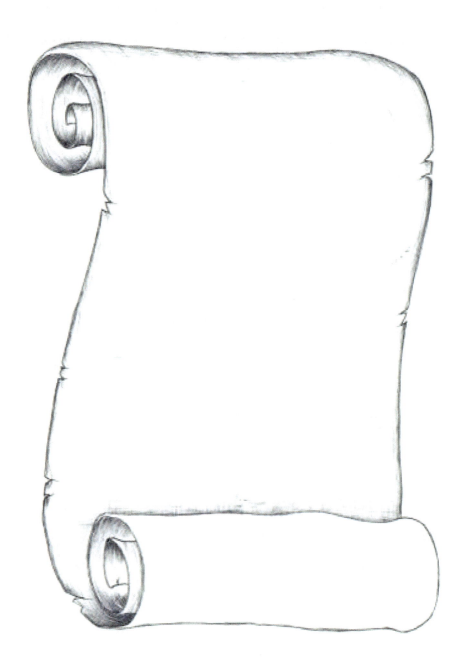

30. OILS

Essential oils have been used for centuries for their therapeutic properties. The Bible mentions several essential oils that were used for healing, including **frankincense, myrrh, cinnamon, cedarwood, spikenard, hyssop**, and **cassia**. In this book, we will explore the therapeutic benefits of these oils specifically for breast cancer patients, including those who have undergone mastectomy.

Frankincense oil is known for its anti-inflammatory and anti-tumor properties. Studies have shown that frankincense oil can induce apoptosis (cell death) in breast cancer cells.
Additionally, it has been found to enhance the efficacy of chemotherapy drugs.

*Myrrh oil i*s another essential oil mentioned in the Bible for its therapeutic properties. It has been found to have anti-tumor effects on breast cancer cells, as well as anti-inflammatory properties.Myrrh oil has also been found to reduce chemotherapy-induced nausea and vomiting. This chapter will explore the benefits of myrrh oil for breast cancer patients.

Cinnamon oil has been found to have anti-cancer properties, including inhibiting the growth of breast cancer cells. It also has anti-inflammatory properties and has been found to improve blood circulation. .

Cedarwood oil has been found to have anti-cancer properties, specifically in inhibiting the growth of breast cancer cells. It also has anti-inflammatory properties and has been found to improve sleep quality.

Spikenard oil has been used for centuries for its medicinal properties. It has been found to have anti-cancer properties and can induce apoptosis in breast cancer cells. Spikenard oil also has anti-inflammatory properties and has been found to reduce stress and anxiety.

Hyssop oil has been used for centuries for its therapeutic properties. It has been found to have anti-inflammatory and anti-tumor properties, including inhibiting the growth of breast cancer cells. Hyssop oil has also been found to have antibacterial properties.

Cassia oil has been found to have anti-cancer properties, specifically in inhibiting the growth of breast cancer cells. It also has anti-inflammatory properties and has been found to improve blood circulation. Cassia oil has also been found to have antibacterial properties.

Not recommendations, merely, my benefits, ***ALWAYS CONSULT YOUR PHYSICIAN AND MEDICAL TEAM!***

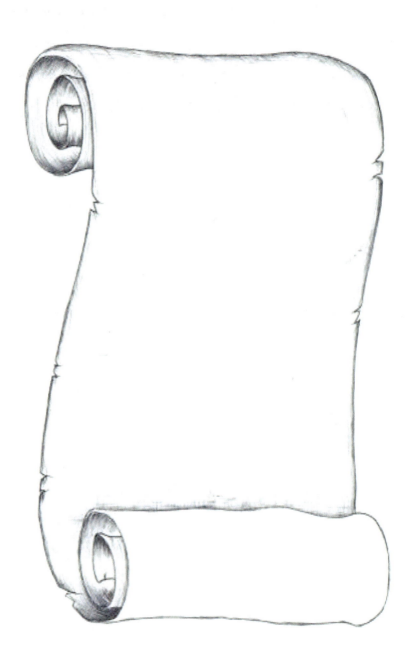

RECIPES

I am not a doctor or a medical professional, and these recipes should not be considered a substitute for proper medical treatment. It's important to consult with a healthcare professional

before making any significant changes to your diet or lifestyle. While no food or drink can cure

breast cancer, maintaining a healthy immune system through a balanced diet can help support

overall well-being. Here are three immune-boosting lemonade recipes that feature ingredients

known for their health-promoting properties:

BERRY GREEN PROTEIN SMOOTHIE

INGREDIENTS

- 1 cup mixed berries (strawberries, blueberries, raspberries, blackberries)

- 1 cup kale (chopped and stems removed)

- 1 cup baby spinach

- 1/2 avocado (ripe, pitted, and peeled)

- 1 tbsp chia seeds

- 1 tbsp ground flaxseed

- 1 scoop (30g) plant-based protein powder (unsweetened or lightly sweetened)

- 1 cup unsweetened almond milk

- 1/2 cup ice

INSTRUCTIONS

1. Wash and prepare the berries, kale, and spinach.

2. Add berries, kale, spinach, avocado, chia seeds, flaxseed, protein powder, almond milk,

and ice to a blender.

3. Blend until smooth, and add more almond milk if needed to achieve desired consistency.

4. Pour into a glass and enjoy immediately.

"Find the strength to face challenges outside your comfort zone."

~Brian Murchinson

"Overcome obstacles no matter the circumstances."

~Sir Stephen Jackson

"You gain strength, courage and confidence facing your fears."

~Zamir Paschal

GINGER TURMERIC PINEAPPLE PROTEIN SMOOTHIE

INGREDIENTS

- 1 cup frozen pineapple chunks

- 1 medium carrot (peeled and chopped)

- 1/2-inch piece of fresh ginger (peeled)

- 1/2-inch piece of fresh turmeric (peeled) or 1/2 tsp ground turmeric

- 1 scoop (30g) plant-based protein powder (unsweetened or lightly sweetened)

- 1 tbsp hemp seeds

- 1 cup coconut water

- 1/2 cup ice

INSTRUCTIONS

1. Prepare the pineapple, carrot, ginger, and turmeric.

2. Add pineapple, carrot, ginger, turmeric, protein powder, hemp seeds, coconut water, and

ice to a blender.

3. Blend until smooth, and add more coconut water if needed to achieve desired

consistency.

4. Pour into a glass and enjoy immediately.

CREAMY CACAO BEET PROTEIN SMOOTHIE

INGREDIENTS

- 1 small beet (cooked, peeled, and chopped)

- 1/2 cup frozen mixed berries

- 1/2 banana

- 1 tbsp raw cacao powder

- 1 tbsp almond butter

- 1 scoop (30g) plant-based protein powder (unsweetened or lightly sweetened)

- 1 tbsp ground flaxseed

- 1 cup unsweetened almond milk

- 1/2 cup ice

INSTRUCTIONS

1. Prepare the beet, mixed berries, and banana.

2. Add beet, mixed berries, banana, cacao powder, almond butter, protein powder, flaxseed,

almond milk, and ice to a blender.

3. Blend until smooth, and add more almond milk if needed to achieve desired consistency.

4. Pour into a glass and enjoy immediately.

Note: These smoothies are not intended to treat or prevent breast cancer, but they contain

nutrients that may help support overall health and immune function. It is important to consult

with a healthcare professional for personalized advice on diet and cancer prevention.

GINGER TURMERIC LEMONADE

INGREDIENTS

- 4 cups water
- 1/2 cup freshly squeezed lemon juice (about 2-3 lemons)
- 2-inch piece fresh ginger, grated
- 1-inch piece fresh turmeric, grated (or 1 tsp turmeric powder)
- 1/4 cup honey or agave syrup
- A pinch of black pepper

INSTRUCTIONS

1. In a small saucepan, bring 2 cups of water to a boil.

2. Add the grated ginger and turmeric (or turmeric powder) to the boiling water.

3. Lower the heat and let it simmer for 10 minutes.

4. Strain the ginger and turmeric mixture into a pitcher.

5. Add the remaining 2 cups of cold water, lemon juice, honey or agave syrup, and a pinch

of black pepper to the pitcher. Stir well.

6. Taste and adjust the sweetness if necessary.

7. Serve over ice and garnish with lemon slices if desired.

BERRY GREEN LEMONADE

INGREDIENTS

- 4 cups water
- 1/2 cup freshly squeezed lemon juice (about 2-3 lemons)
- 1 cup mixed berries (e.g. strawberries, blueberries, raspberries)
- 2 cups fresh spinach or kale, washed and stems removed
- 1/4 cup honey or agave syrup

INSTRUCTIONS

1. In a blender, combine the mixed berries and spinach or kale. Blend until smooth.

2. Strain the berry and green mixture through a fine mesh sieve or cheesecloth to remove

any pulp and seeds.

3. In a pitcher, combine the strained berry and green mixture with the water, lemon juice,

and honey or agave syrup. Stir well.

4. Taste and adjust the sweetness if necessary.

5. Serve over ice and garnish with additional berries if desired.

CHIA SEED LEMONADE

INGREDIENTS

- 4 cups water

- 1/2 cup freshly squeezed lemon juice (about 2-3 lemons)

- 1/4 cup honey or agave syrup

- 1/4 cup chia seeds

- Optional: 1/2 cup fresh mint leaves

INSTRUCTIONS

1. In a pitcher, combine the water, lemon juice, and honey or agave syrup. Stir well.

2. Add the chia seeds and stir until well distributed.

3. If using mint leaves, gently bruise them with your fingers to release their oils and add

them to the pitcher.

4. Refrigerate the lemonade for at least 1 hour, allowing the chia seeds to expand and form

a gel-like texture.

5. Stir the lemonade before serving to redistribute the chia seeds.

6. Serve over ice and garnish with lemon slices and additional mint leaves if desired.

30 QUOTES FOR YOU

1. "I have been through a lot, and I've realized the importance of living each day to the fullest." - Sheryl Crow

2. "Cancer may have started the fight, but I will finish it." - Elizabeth Edwards

3. "I have breast cancer; it doesn't have me." - Donna Brazile

4. "Cancer is a word, not a sentence." - Wynonna Judd

5. "The most important thing in illness is never to lose heart." - Nikolai Lenin

6. "When life kicks you, let it kick you forward." - Kay Yow

7. "You gain strength, courage, and confidence by every experience in which you really stop

to look fear in the face." - Eleanor Roosevelt

8. "It's about focusing on the fight and not the fright." - Robin Roberts

9. "Life is not over because you have breast cancer. Make the most of what you have; be

grateful." - Dale Evans

10. "The most important thing in life is to stop saying 'I wish' and start saying 'I will'. Consider nothing is impossible, then treat possibilities as probabilities." - Charles Dickens

11. "My scars remind me that I am still here and that I am still fighting." - Sarah Williams

12. "I'm still alive, and that's all that counts." - Kylie Minogue

13. "Never, never, never give up." - Winston Churchill

14. "Once you choose hope, anything is possible." - Christopher Reeve

15. "The most important thing is to have a positive attitude." - Coco Chanel

16. "I may have had cancer, but cancer never had me." - Marissa Jaret Winokur

17. "You never know how strong you are until being strong is the only choice you have." - Bob Marley.

18. "I have cancer, but it doesn't have me." - Christina Applegate

19. "Cancer may have started the fight, but I will finish it." - Christie Brinkley

20. "I learned that courage was not the absence of fear, but the triumph over it." - Nelson Mandela

21. "A cancer diagnosis is not a death sentence, but a call to life."

-Bernadette Tuazon

22. "I have been given a second chance at life, and I intend to use it to the fullest." - Melissa Etheridge

23. "I don't think of myself as a victim. I think of myself as a survivor."

- Geri Halliwell

24. "Breast cancer changes you, and the change can be beautiful."

 - Jane Cook

25. "There is always something to be thankful for." - Rhonda Byrne

26. "I believe that every single event in life happens in an opportunity to choose love over

fear." - Oprah Winfrey

27. "Don't wait for something big to occur. Start where you are, with what you have, and that

will always lead you into something greater." - Mary Manin Morrissey

28. "Your life is your story. Write well. Edit often." - Susan Statham

29. "Life is too short to waste time on things that don't matter." - Jenna Morasca

30. "The best way to predict your future is to create it." - Abraham Lincoln.

EPILOGUE

After months of enduring grueling treatments, emotional upheaval, and physical pain, a woman emerged from her battle with breast cancer victorious. I faced my greatest fears head-on and in order to come out on the other side with a newfound appreciation for life.

My journey has been long and arduous, but it taught me invaluable lessons about myself and the world around me. I discovered a strength within myself that I never knew existed while also learning to trust and to rely on the support of those around me.

As I closed the book on my first battle with breast cancer, I looked forward to a future filled with hope and possibility. I knew that life would never be the same again, but I was grateful for the chance to embrace every moment, to cherish the people I loved, and those that love me in order to make the most of every opportunity that comes my way.

My hope and desire is that my story serves as a reminder to others that even in the darkest of times, there is always hope. With determination, courage, and the support of loved ones, anything is possible.

RESOURCES

The American Cancer Society: provides resources for women with breast cancer, including information on treatment options, support groups, and programs for
financial assistance. BreastCancer.org: This website provides information on breast cancer diagnosis, treatment, and survivorship. It also offers support forums and a helpline. Susan G. Komen: Susan G. Komen is a nonprofit organization dedicated to breast cancer research and advocacy. They offer resources for women with breast cancer, including support groups, treatment information, and educational materials.

Living Beyond Breast Cancer: is a nonprofit organization dedicated to providing support and resources for women with breast cancer. They offer
webinars, support groups, and educational materials.

CancerCare: CancerCare provides free support services for individuals affected by cancer, including counseling, support groups, and financial assistance.

The Breast Cancer Research Foundation: The Breast Cancer Research Foundation is a nonprofit organization dedicated to funding research for the prevention and cure of breast

cancer. They also offer educational materials and resources for women with breast cancer.

National Cancer Institute: The National Cancer Institute provides information on breast cancer diagnosis, treatment, and research. They also offer clinical trials for new breast cancer treatments.

Cancer Support Community: The Cancer Support Community provides resources and support for individuals with cancer, including support groups, counseling, and educational materials.

Young Survival Coalition: The Young Survival Coalition is a nonprofit organization dedicated to providing support and resources for young women with breast cancer. They offer support groups, educational materials, and advocacy services.

Breast Cancer Action: Breast Cancer Action is a nonprofit organization dedicated to advocating for women with breast cancer. They offer information on breast cancer treatment and prevention, as well as advocacy services.

National Comprehensive Cancer Network: The National

Comprehensive Cancer Network provides guidelines for the treatment of

breast cancer. They also offer information on clinical trials and research.

Breast Cancer Now: Breast Cancer Now is a UK-based charity

that provides information and support for women with breast cancer.

They offer a helpline, online forums, and educational

materials.

FORCE: Facing Our Risk of Cancer Empowered (FORCE)

provides support and resources for women with hereditary breast and

ovarian cancer. They offer support groups, educational materials, and

advocacy services.

The Pink Fund: The Pink Fund provides financial assistance for

women with breast cancer who are experiencing financial hardship. They

offer assistance with bills, rent/mortgage payments, and other expenses.

National Breast Cancer Coalition: The National Breast Cancer

Coalition is a nonprofit

organization dedicated to ending breast cancer. They offer advocacy

services and resources for

women with breast cancer.

Cancer and Careers: Cancer and Careers provides resources and support for individuals with cancer who are working or looking to return to work. They offer career counseling, webinars, and educational materials.

Sharsheret: Sharsheret is a nonprofit organization dedicated to providing support and resources for Jewish women with breast cancer. They offer support groups, educational materials, and advocacy services.

Breast Friends: Breast Friends is a nonprofit organization dedicated to providing emotional support for women with breast cancer. They offer support groups, educational materials, and retreats.

MyLifeLine: MyLifeLine provides online support and resources for individuals with cancer. They offer personalized websites for cancer patients, as well as support groups and educational materials.

REFERENCES:

Bennett, M.P., Zeller, J.M., Rosenberg, L., & McCann, J. (2003). The effect of mirthful laughter on stress and natural killer cell activity. Alternative Therapies in Health and Medicine, 9(2), 38-45.

Berk, L.S., Tan, S.A., Fry, W.F., Napier, B.J., Lee, J.W., Hubbard, R.W., ... & Eby, W.C. (1989). Neuroendocrine and stress hormone changes during mirthful laughter. The American Journal of the Medical Sciences, 298(6), 390-396.

Dunbar, R.I.M., Baron, R., Frangou, A., Pearce, E., van Leeuwen, E.J.C., Stow, J., ... & van Vugt, M. (2012). Social laughter is correlated with an elevated pain threshold. Proceedings of the Royal Society B: Biological Sciences, 279(1731), 1161-1167.

Gelkopf, M., Kreitler, S., & Sigal, M. (1997). Laughter in a psychiatric ward: Somatic, emotional, social, and clinical influences on schizophrenic patients. Journal of Nervous and Mental Disease, 185(5), 283-289.

"Courage is the moral strength to overcome life's hardships and uncertainties."

~Desiree' Jackson

"Don't talk about it, be about it... Take the fucking hill!"

~US Army SFC Adrian White

"Be brave and able to do something you haven't done before."

~Jaizzy Waizzy Dyton (Prince Jai)

"Courage is jumping from the plane, understanding the trials of letting go, yet the thrill and faith of finding the unknown. Face to face with yourself, putting all your hard work to the test."

~Norman Anthony Ross

ACKNOWLEDGMENTS

Embarking on this journey, I was privileged to be surrounded by an extraordinary creative team whose dedication was unparalleled. Each one of you brought unique gifts and talents to the table, showing unwavering commitment through what often proved to be exhaustive and rigorous cycles of creation. The countless days and nights we spent together, fueled by sheer determination, were testimony to our collective zeal.

Translating an abstract vision into tangible form is no small feat, and it was evident that the process demanded immense patience. There were moments marked by repetitive edits, where my thoughts were a maze, yet you navigated with precision, constantly fine-tuning to ensure the final product mirrored the initial concept residing in my mind.

I would be remiss not to convey my heartfelt gratitude for the tireless efforts, the endless patience, and the ceaseless belief you all showed in this endeavor. Each of you, in your own special way, contributed to making this dream a reality, and for that, I am eternally thankful.

David Manion,

Thank you for the scrolls! Your artwork and vision captured my heart and dreams... Destiny! Warmest Wishes, Lolita

Dominic Harris,

As one of the foremost talents in graphic and web design, your dedication and expertise have been instrumental. Despite the challenges and moments of ambiguity, you consistently navigated the complexities of my vision, translating it into reality with grace and precision. Your unwavering professionalism, combined with your exceptional talents, set a standard that the industry greatly benefits from.

I express my profound gratitude to you for all your contributions. I also extend my warm regards to your family. Thank you, Dominic, and I anticipate witnessing even greater achievements from you in the future.

Sincerely, Lolita

Dariana Badillo,

Your exceptional skills, remarkable talents, and enduring patience are a testament to your profound expertise in graphic artistry. From our very first meeting, I recognized the unique and innate creativity you possess. I am deeply appreciative of the assistance you offered when I was in dire need of it. The world undoubtedly awaits the continued showcase of your capabilities. Additionally, I fondly reminisce about our times together and would like to extend my gratitude to your family for their trust in our friendship, and professional relationship. Please convey my warm regards to your parents. Thank you for everything, Dariana.

Sincerely, Lolita

Joe Ferrara,

Though we were once unfamiliar to each other, your unwavering faith in my vision was evident from our earliest interactions. I am deeply appreciative of your commitment to the mission and your decision to join this journey with me. Your entrance into my professional life came during a particularly challenging phase, marked by scattered projects and incomplete designs. However, with your exceptional skills in Mechanical Product Design, Web Design, and CAD Engineering, combined with patience and finesse, you adeptly guided me through the complexities. Your contributions are invaluable, and I sincerely thank you for all you've done.

Warm regards, Lolita

Ms. Ma'Leah Miller,

It is with sincere appreciation that I acknowledge your invaluable contribution to the completion of this book. Your patience, sensitivity, and exceptional expertise were precisely what this project required. I am deeply grateful for your unparalleled professionalism and the wealth of knowledge you bring as a renowned author of three books, a freelance writer, and an educator. Concurrently pursuing your Master's Degree in Education further underscores your unwavering dedication and commitment to excellence."

Sincerely, Lolita

Stephen Jackson,

Your unwavering support has been the cornerstone of my journey. You are more than just a friend or husband to me; you are my anchor and my most trusted confidant. Without you by my side, I couldn't have become the resilient individual I needed to be in the face of such adversity. Our journey has been challenging, testing the very depths of our resilience. Together, we faced the trials, comforting and strengthening each other through the sleepless nights and shared tears.

Your dedication and sacrifice, through every high and low, serve as a testament to the profound bond we share. Each time I look into your eyes, I'm reminded of the blessing and the divine love that brought us together. You deserve the world and all its joys, and as long as I'm by your side, I will do my utmost to ensure you experience the happiness and fulfillment you've so selflessly afforded me. Stephen, I deeply value and cherish everything you've done for us. Now, it's time for you to embrace the tranquility and joy you've earned. My gratitude for you is boundless, and my love for you is eternal.

With deepest affection, Lolita."

Dear Toot,

I am writing you this letter to let you know just how much I love you. I'm sitting here thinking

about my diagnosis, family, children, and you being my first born has me contemplating back to

the day that you were born…

I think about being in labor for three days waiting for you to get here. I remember everything

about the labor experience, being in the hospital, in the hospital room along with all of our family

members and hearing mom tell the nurses and family over and over that they needed to take

you out of me. Well, they did! You were such a beautiful baby boy, 8 pounds 4 ounces! I had to

have surgery to bring you into the world and I'm having to have surgery again dealing with

another set of circumstances.

I love you Toot, you were such a smart baby, you could read completely at two years old. Your hair was long, curly and beautiful. Your skin was sun kissed. You are still the same way, smart, beautiful with the world ahead of you. Now it's your turn to go make

some beautiful babies and

enjoy your life!

Loving you more than forever, and forever more I'll always love you...

Your mother,

Lolita

My Dearest Howard Howard Howard (Johnny Wanny)

I was thinking about you today, wondering what you're doing? How is life treating you? Lately, I've had a lot on my mind to say the least, but you and your brothers and sister have been at the forefront of my thoughts. I was thinking about when you were born, I knew that I had to have a

c-section in advance and I wanted things to be entirely different for your birth . I wanted to be

awake so that I didn't miss a thing…

I remember the operating room being really cold, and I could feel a lot of pulling, I was groggy,

your dad was in the room with me, I couldn't see what they were doing but I did feel this pulling

sensation and the next thing I knew there was commotion and they showed me a baby over the

makeshift sheet blocker saying it's a boy! I thought to myself, o no, what about all of that pink

stuff I bought for the baby. I remember you were screaming to the top of your lungs... It truly

was incredible and remarkable for me to experience and witness.

212

When they showed you to me, your skin was covered in blood, and goop, you had a

white/purple skin color and you were crying, crying, crying. I thought to myself, he's such a

beautiful baby, o my. I told your dad that you looked like your Uncle Scott with my eyes! Your

Dad was so proud, smiling from ear to ear.

I want you to know how much I love you, always have and always will. You were the kindest,

loving baby, young man, and now man.

Howard, you're smart, you're wise, you go deep, that brain of yours is remarkable, you're a

thinker, it's been incredible to witness.

Now, go have lots of babies and pass that onto your children...

I love you, Howard... Always and Forever,

Your mom, Lolita

P.S. Do you realize you always say, "Mom?" It's so funny I miss it when I don't hear it!

Thank You, Thank You, Thank You, to all my family

and friends for your support and love!

Loving you more than forever,

and forever more, I'll always love you...

~Lolita

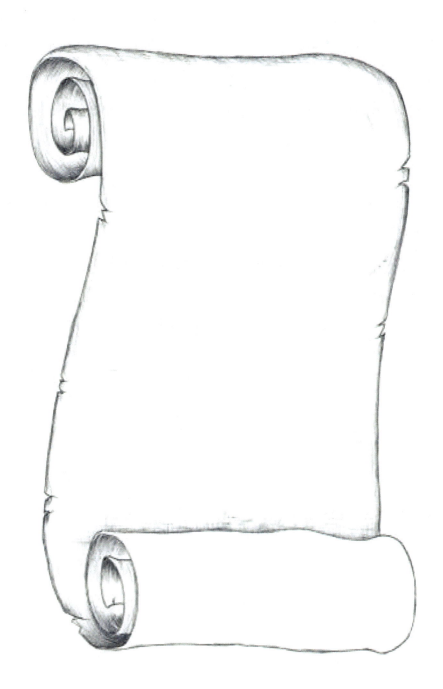

Made in the USA
Monee, IL
11 September 2023

42472071R00122